THE NEW
POMERANIAN

by

Sari Brewster Tietjen

First Edition

HOWELL
BOOK HOUSE
New York

Howell Book House
Macmillan Publishing Company
866 Third Avenue, New York, NY 10022
Collier Macmillan Canada, Inc.

Library of Congress Cataloging-in-Publication Data

Tietjen, Sari Brewster.
  The new Pomeranian.

Bibliography: p. 191.

  1. Pomeranian dogs.   I. Title.
SF429.P8T54   1987   636.7′6   87-22823
ISBN 0-87605-251-0

Macmillan books are available at special discounts for bulk purchases for sales promotions, premiums, fund-raising, or educational use. For details, contact:

Special Sales Director
Macmillan Publishing Company
866 Third Avenue
New York, NY 10022

10 9 8 7 6 5 4 3

Printed in the United States of America

For

my mother, Mary S. Brewster
and
my sister, Joy S. Brewster

Long-time Pomeranian breeders and aficionados

Etruscan coin of Roman Empire, dated 210
B.C., depicting small Pomeranian type dog.

Head study of a Dutch champion male, Unique van het Pinneland, owned and bred by
Mrs. Saes-Vaessen, Holland.

Contents

Sari Brewster Tietjen

The Tom Reynolds Studio

Acknowledgments

IN ORDER FOR a book about a specific breed to be viable and useful to members of the dog fancy, it must reach across a broad spectrum of dog owners. This book on the Pomeranian was designed with both the dedicated breeder and the individual pet owner in mind. It contains something for everyone.

No writer of any breed book can do justice to a breed without the guidance and assistance of others. I am deeply indebted to a lot of people who generously gave of their time and expertise to help me with this project. My mother, Mary S. Brewster (Robwood Kennels), and my sister, Joy S. Brewster (Cassio Kennels), Pomeranian breeders of long standing, answered a myriad of questions. Noted artist Roy Andersen painted the beautiful cover portrait of one of my sister's dogs, Ch. Fun Fair's Pinto O'Joe Dandy. Chris Heartz volunteered to draw the exquisite ink sketchings of positive and negative breed points. Jessie and Barbara Young wrote of the perceptive obedience hints and prompted quick English assistance. William Ledbetter, my German contact, shared his interest and knowledge of color genetics. Sophie Mayes, a former *Review* editor, wrote the marvelous article on line/in/cross breeding and guided me towards Elma Maines' basic whelping article.

I owe thanks to Olga and Darrell Baker, whose enthusiasm for this project was unsurpassed; Susan Buckel, for her piece on training the show dog; Porter Washington, for sharing Sparky's story; and Sally Baugniet, for her input on various breed topics. Anna LaFortune wrote the practical tips on whelping and raising puppies, and Forrest and May McCoy contributed to the section on grooming and trimming.

Ina Kniffin, Edna Girarodot, Dorothy Bonner, Isodore Schoenberg are some of the many long-time Pom breeders who offered special assistance. English friends Ann Winter and Derek Hill, Carry Saes from Holland, and German breeders Eyke Schmidt-Rohde, Mrs. Waltraud Omlin and Karl Busse all graciously offered insight and photographs covering the present-day Pomeranian in Europe. Various other Pomeranian breeders also came forth with source materials.

John Ashbey, a wonderful American photographer, took the before and after trimming shots, allowed us to reprint some of his portrait photographs and dug out old photographs of his father, Frank Ashbey, a Pomeranian handler. Fox & Cook are responsible for the photos of Dick Hammond's paintings. Pom owner and photographer Pam Welsh, Ed Jenner, Roberta Massey, Phyliss Suby, Diane Johnson, Jackie Liddle, Sherry and Earl Steinmetz, Gladys Dkystra and Rosalind Golts are but some of the Pom owners who sent photographs of their dogs.

Thanks are also due to Her Majesty Queen Elizabeth II and the British Royal Family for their excellent collection of paintings and photographs; Miss Pamela Clark of the Royal Archives, who uncovered valuable Pomeranian history; Miss Dimond of the Royal Photographs; the Tate Gallery and Frick Museum, as well as Richard Hammond. All contributed promptly to the quest for art pieces.

Roberta Vesley, librarian at the American Kennel Club, personally delved through countless books and materials; the College of William and Mary and the Vassar College Library provided additional resource materials.

At last, but by no means least, a special thank you to Howell Book House—the late Elsworth S. Howell, who encouraged me to write this book, as well as Seymour Weiss, Sean Frawley and their staff. To my husband Herman and son Rick, and our Japanese Chins—thanks for all the patience, support and understanding.

Sari B. Tietjen
Rhinebeck, New York

Queen Charlotte, wife of England's King George III, brought Pomeranians with her from Germany when she married the soon-to-be-crowned King in 1761. Pomeranians remained as pets of her court and she gave several to peers. This portrait of Queen Charlotte, which features a small white Pom seated at the Queen's right, was painted by Stroehling, a noted portrait painter of the day.

From the Collection of Her Majesty the Queen

1

From Whence a Name

My Lord,

When last I saw you at Windsor you expressed a fondness for the Pommeranian Dogs. I wrote to Germany and have received this morning from Pomerania through the means of GZ. Freyborg two Pair, of which I now offer two in Truth very beautifull for that Species their Names, Mercury and Phebe. May I also give you a hint, that they ought not to be sent in the Square, for being the true breed they may become a temptation for Dog Steelers. I shall be glad to hear that they afford you some pleasure which may perhaps be the case, for the messenger says, that they are young and clever at learning tricks.

Charlotte

THIS LETTER, from Queen Charlotte, wife of England's King George III, to Lord Harcourt, one of the King's governors, was dated November 28, 1767 and accompanies two young canines whom the Queen referred to as Pommeranian Dogs. Queen Charlotte had procured the dogs from Pomerania, a principality in the northeastern corner of what is presently known as

"The Prince of Wales' Phaeton" by George Stubbs (1793) shows Fino, the Prince's pet Pomeranian, greeting a horse.

From the Collection of Her Majesty the Queen

George Stubbs' "Fino and Tiny" (179-) features the Prince's black and white Pom with a small King Charles Spaniel trying to get him to play.

From the Collection of Her Majesty the Queen

"The Mall at St. James' Park" (1783?) is a lovely casual painting depicting groups of ladies strolling in a park setting accompanied by their small dogs. The white dog to the right is a Pomeranian, while the one to the left is a King Charles. The center animal is open for speculation. The Frick Collection, New York.   *Gainsborough*

"Pomeranian Bitch and Puppy" (1777) was reputed to have been painted by Gainsborough in exchange for music lessons. The Tate Museum, London.

Gainsborough

13

East Germany. The Queen, who was only 17 years of age when she entered into a politically expedient marriage with the yet to be crowned George III, came from the duchy of Mecklenburg, a neighbor of Pomerania. Her introduction of the Pomeranian to England more than likely dates the breed's first official entry into Great Britain, and references what has become known as the accepted breed name, although the double "mm" was later dropped.

Queen Charlotte and King George III had 15 children, two of whom died in infancy. The royal couple, known for simple habits and tastes and a deep concern for home and family life, were frequently surrounded with a variety of animals. The Pomeranians of Queen Charlotte's court were large, often weighing from 20 to 30 pounds, and coarser in head and bone than the popular Poms of today. Most of the dogs were white or cream in color. One exception was "Fino," a particular pet of the Queen's son, the Prince of Wales who later became King George IV. George Stubbs (1724–1806), a fashionable animal artist, painted two well-known paintings in which "Fino" was depicted. One, titled "The Prince of Wales' Phaeton" (1793), shows Fino positioned on his hindlegs greeting the carriage; the other, designated "Fino and Tiny" (179–), has the black and white Pomeranian standing beside a King Charles Spaniel. Another exception is portrayed in an earlier Stubbs' portrait, "A Pomeranian Dog" (1773), where the coarse, top-heavy, Spitz-type dog is reddish brown in color.

White Poms were the norm. Thomas Gainsborough (1728–1788) was very fond of the dogs and used them in several paintings. Three of particular interest are: (1) "Mrs. Robinson with a White Fox Dog" (1781–82)—Mrs. Robinson was an actress who was reputed to have been an early mistress of the Prince of Wales; (2) "The Mall in St. James' Park" (1783?)—a strolling group of lovely ladies, of whom the three center women were said to be daughters of King George III, accompanied by three small lap dogs, of which one is a white Pomeranian; and (3) "Pomeranian Bitch and Puppy" (1777)—a lovely portrait of two dogs belonging to C. F. Abel, a noted musician of the period. It has been written that Gainsborough painted this portrait in return for viola de gamba lessons.

2

Early History

AS PREVIOUSLY STATED, the naming territory for the Pomeranian was established as Pomerania. This region, bordered on the north by the Baltic Sea, had been at various times under the control of the Celts, Slavonic tribes, Poland, Sweden, Denmark and Prussia. The name *Pomore,* or *Pommern,* meaning "on the sea," was given to the district about the time of Charlemagne. A bay, called the Gulf of Pomerania in Poland and Pomeranian Bay in Germany, touches lands of both Pomerania in East Germany and various provinces of present-day Poland.

The people of coastal Pomerania were dependent on the sea and frequently engaged in trading with the inhabitants of Scandinavian countries to their north and the remainder of the European continent to the south. Using the waterways to trade goods between territories, the traders were often accompanied by dogs, who served as workers, companions or merchandise to be bartered. One particular group of the dogs utilized in this fashion has been classified as dogs belonging to the northern group—"dogs derived mainly from the northern wolf (canis lupus), comprising the huskies, samoyeds, chows, pomeranians, elkhounds, collies, alsatians,

CHAPTER IV.

ON THE VARIETIES OF THE DOG.

WE now venture to offer the following as an arrangement of the principal breeds into which the domestic dog appears to be resolvable; from this arrangement we exclude the true wild dogs of India and the dingo of Australia, but retain in it such dogs as have reverted to a life of independence, and which may be termed feral:—

1. Ears, erect or nearly so; nose, pointed; hair, long, often woolly; form, robust and muscular; aspect, more or less wolfish.

> Feral dog of Russia.
> Feral dog of Natolia.
> Shepherd's dog of Natolia.
> Persian guard dog.
> Pomeranian dog.
> Icelandish dog.
> Siberian dog.
> Tschuktschi dog.
> Esquimaux dog.
> Hare Indian dog. [dians.
> Black wolf-dog of Florida In-
> Nootka dog.
> Shepherd dog.

2. Ears, narrow, semi-erect, or only slightly pendulous; muzzle, produced; jaws, strong; hair, smooth or wiry; limbs, long and vigorous; power of scent, not highly developed.

> Ancient German hoarhound, the Sau-ruden of Redinger.
> Great Danish dog.
> Feral dog of Hayti.
> French mâtin.
> Irish wolf-dog.
> Scotch deerhound.
> English greyhound.
> Italian greyhound.
> Persian greyhound.
> Brinjaree dog.
> Albanian greyhound.
> Lurcher.

3. Ears, moderately large and pendent; muzzle, deep and strong; hair, long, sometimes wiry; form, robust; aspect, grave and intelligent.

> Italian wolf-dog.
> Newfoundland dog.
> Labrador dog.
> Alpine dog.

4. Ears, moderately large; sometimes very large, pendent; hair, long and fine; muzzle, moderate; forehead, developed; scent, acute; intelligence at a high ratio.

> Spaniel and fancy varieties.
> Water-spaniel and varieties.
> Rough water-dog or barbet.
> Little barbet.
> Setter.

5. Ears, large, pendent; muzzle, long and deep; nose, large; hair, close; scent, acute; form, vigorous.

> Pointer.
> Dalmatian dog.
> Beagle.
> Harrier.
> Foxhound.
> Old English hound.
> Bloodhound.
> African hound, &c.

6. Ears, moderate, pendent; muzzle, short and thick; jaws, enormously strong; hair, short, sometimes wiry; form, robust; sense of smell variable.

> Cuban mastiff.
> English mastiff.
> Thibet mastiff.
> Bandog.
> Bulldog.
> Corsican and Spanish bulldog.
> Pug-dog.

7. Ears, sub-erect; muzzle, rather acute; jaws, strong; hair, short or wiry; scent, acute; habits, active; intelligence, considerable.

> Terrier — smooth and wire-haired.
> Turnspit.
> Barbary dog.

We do not offer this arrangement, which is essentially the same as that which we have elsewhere given, as not liable to objections; indeed so many mixed breeds of dogs of uncertain origin exist, that any attempt to class them under distinct heads would appear hopeless. We must confess, however, that F. Cuvier's arrangement of

Chart of 1845 varietal characteristics for canines in 7 categories. The Pomeranian is specifically mentioned in category 1.

16

corgis, schipperkes and terriers." The dogs had been domesticated and trained for the work required of them. Territorial centers were established, functioning with whatever ancestral stocks were available and forming a variety of dogs with anatomically similar makeup, yet possessing many different characteristics.

The general anatomical categorization of the northern group of dogs includes: "ears, erect or nearly so; nose, pointed; hair, long often wooly; form, robust and muscular; aspect, more or less wolfish." In his illustrated chart, W.C.L. Martin, author of *The History of the Dog: Its Origin, Physical and Moral Characteristics, and Its Principal Varieties* (London, 1845), suggests that there were seven old general categories of varietal characteristics for canines. The Pomeranian breed was specifically mentioned as belonging to the first category or northern group.

Structure frequently varied as different breed characteristics within the group became dominant and protected through careful line breeding of type to type. Hence, today we have the Alaskan Malamute, Keeshond, Schipperke and the Pomeranian—to name but four present day representative types of the northern group. These breeds are also sometimes classified as Spitz dogs.

The Spitz-type dog—or northern group type, whichever classification name you prefer—is quite old. Dogs with these general characteristics appear on Grecian tablets and vases that dated to 400 B.C. The smaller varieties were favorite pets of wealthy ladies and their children. The larger, sturdier dogs were popular as haulers of goods and supplies, watchdogs and guardians, and were sometimes employed as flock watchers.

It is the smaller variety that developed into the present-day Pomeranian. The gradual acceptance by the well-to-do and nobility on the European continent of these companionable, active dogs meant an increased tendency to breed the Spitz-type dog down in size. The person often given credit by many sources for advocating and publicizing the trend toward acceptance of the smaller Pom is Great Britain's Queen Victoria.

Queen Victoria holds in her arms her pet Pom, Turi, as she rides a carriage in Dublin, Ireland in April of 1900. Within a year, she was dead. One of her last wishes was for Turi to be brought to her bed for comforting. Photograph Collection of Her Majesty the Queen.   *Cartland*

Late 1800s English painter, Francis L. Fairman, painted this portrait of four black English Pomeranians, dated 1895. From the collection of Richard Hammond.
Fox & Cook

18

3

A Queen's Patronage

ALTHOUGH POMERANIANS were first introduced to English nobility by Queen Charlotte, it was her granddaughter—Queen Victoria—who, some hundred years later, had the biggest impact on promoting the breed and encouraging its popularity.

Victoria's rule over the British empire for 64 years is commonly known as the Victorian Era, a time of great progress as well as wastefulness, opulence and extravagance. Under Queen Victoria's reign, Britain expanded both within and without to faraway commonwealth territories in India, South Africa and China. The children and grandchildren of the Queen became the monarchs who ruled all Europe. In her later years, Queen Victoria was known as the "Granny-Gran" of the continent.

England's longest reigning monarch had a complex and diversified personality. During her 82 years, she underwent four evolutionary changes: from an overly sheltered and protected child to a chaste girl-queen; from a subservient wife and monarch to a much admired, eccentric matriarch, ruler of a vast realm.

Always at the side of the benevolent Queen were her favorite four-footed companions. She cherished all animals, but dogs could be considered her closest allies. They enveloped her lifestyle and that of her court. No matter how grave governmental affairs may have been, nor the capriciousness of private family outings, her dogs were invariably present.

During Victoria's lifetime, she enjoyed the company of more than 15 different breeds. They encompassed the majestic sighthounds, gentle retrievers, watchful shepherd's dogs, terriers and the lap dogs. Among the breeds she patronized were Pomeranians, Italian Greyhounds, Pekingese, Pugs, Toy Spaniels, Skye Terriers, Dandie Dinmont Terriers, Fox Terriers, St. Bernards, Collies, Bloodhounds, Dachshunds, Beagles, Otter Hounds, Deerhounds and Greyhounds. Her family also maintained a prevailing interest in many of these and additional breeds, including Basset Hounds, Borzois, Newfoundlands and Japanese Spaniels.

Her Majesty always believed that people should love their pets "not wisely, but too well," and should let the animals be a source of happiness. When her husband, Prince Albert, passed away unexpectedly in 1861 at the age of 42, she turned to her pets for solace. With the Prince Consort gone, she developed closer ties to her animals and took an in-depth interest in new breeds, adding more dogs from different breeds to her menagerie.

While touring the Mediterranean in 1888, Queen Victoria found in Florence, Italy, a mid-size Pomeranian, weighing approximately 12 pounds, and brought him home. Although her grandmother, Queen Charlotte, and her uncle, King George IV, had owned Poms, the breed never passed on to Victoria's branch of the Royal Family. Queen Charlotte predeceased her granddaughter by a year, dying in 1818, and King George IV died when the future Queen was a much sheltered 11 year old. The large, white dogs that Queen Charlotte had called Pommeranians never attained lasting popularity.

Queen Victoria's interest in Poms, however, excited the general populace, as the Queen had become a much beloved monarch whose every move was chronicled and copied. By this time, her concern for dogs had already been documented and the country was eager to accept her latest specimens.

"Marco" (1893), by Burton Barber. Queen Victoria brought Marco from Italy and he has been credited by many for starting the trend toward smaller Pomeranians in England.
From the Collection of Her Majesty the Queen

The dogs in "Marco with Snowball and Janey" (1893) were three of Queen Victoria's pets painted by noted animal painter, Burton Barber. Snowball is the large white Scotch Collie, while Marco and Janey were two of the Queen's Pomeranians. Photograph courtesy of the Courtauld Institute of Art.
From the Collection of Her Majesty the Queen

The dog from Florence was called "Marco" and he quickly became a royal housepet. English dog shows were still in their infancy and the Queen had several of her dogs shown at local London events. When members of the Royal Family entered their dogs in shows, they increased public interest not only in their animals but also in dog shows and dog ownership. Most of their wins were reported in London newspapers for public consumption. "Windsor Marco's" show career was avidly reported and he was described as being "a deep red sable colour with tail and hind featherings of a very pale tint of the same hue, almost white."

Charles Henry Lane, a prominent English dog show judge, wrote about a visit to Queen Victoria's Pomeranian kennel in Windsor in his book *All About Dogs* (1912):

> Pomeranians are seemingly popular with all classes, from Royalty downward. Her Majesty the Queen has a large kennel of them at Windsor, which I had the honour of an invitation to inspect, and can testify to the great interest taken in the breed, and the number of specimens kept, with every care and consideration shown for their happiness and comfort. Her Majesty's collection, when I saw them, some time since, consisted almost entirely of what I should call "off colours," that is, not white, black, brown or blue, but shades and mixtures of those and other colours, some exceedingly pretty, and although somewhat larger in size, being mostly "small-medium," and not so fine in head as many of the dogs now shown, are so good in other respects, that they have often successfully competed with well-known specimens, when Her Majesty has entered any at the Royal Agricultural Hall and Crystal Palace Shows.

In the same book, Mr. Lane recalls the first time he judged any of Queen Victoria's dogs:

> I remember it so happened that the first time Her Majesty the Queen exhibited any dogs, nearly all Her Majesty's entries came into my classes at a Great London show. Soon after my entering the building I went to have a look at my classes, and shortly afterwards, the secretary came up to me and said, "Do you know you have the great honour of being the first man to judge any dogs from Her Majesty's kennels?"

I said, "I have heard so."

He then said, "Well, I am most anxious they should be in the prize list, as I consider it a high honour that Her Majesty has allowed them to be entered."

I said, "That is all right enough, but although I will not admit Her Majesty has a more loyal or devoted subject than myself, I am here in a public capacity as a judge, and if Her Majesty's dogs are entered, in competition with Her Majesty's subjects' dogs, they can only be judged 'on their merits,' and from what I can see on the benches as the Royal dogs have been pointed out to me by your keepers I don't think many of them will be 'in the money,' as the classes are very large and good."

He said, "That will never do; what can be done?"

I said, "Will you leave it to me?"

He said, "Yes, entirely."

I said, "Then I will have all the dogs of the same colour and type as those from the Royal kennels formed into a separate class (which luckily, was feasible) and judged together."

This was done and I hoped caused general satisfaction, which would not have been the case had any partiality been shown, nor would such have been approved by Her Majesty, I am perfectly sure, if the circumstances became to be known at the palace.

Was the breed Mr. Lane judged the Pomeranian? He does not say, but there were several colors and sizes of Poms presented at shows during that time and splitting classes would not have been hard. It is not difficult to imagine what it must have been like to not only judge the Queen's dogs, but to exhibit against them as well. Fortunately, Queen Victoria's interest had a positive effect on the little Poms, as the breed was now in Britain to stay and improve. The 12 pounders that the Queen favored over the earlier 20- to 30-pound specimens of Charlotte's era soon gave way to a more fashionable, smaller still (under eight-pound) dog and the Toy Pomeranian was born in England.

Some years before Queen Victoria acquired her first Pomeranian, she came across one in India. The dog so impressed her that she wrote the following as her daily journal entry of August 17, 1881:

At 11, I gave six good conduct medals to Sergeants & Corporals, who had, all but one, been in the 66th Regt. in the dreadful retreat, after

Two three-month-old puppies, Lina and Beppo, were also brought by the Queen from Florence, Italy in 1888. Photograph Collection of Her Majesty the Queen.

Cartland

Gina was nine months old when Queen Victoria brought her to London from Italy in 1888. She went on to win prizes for the Queen at London dog shows. Photograph Collection of Her Majesty the Queen.

24

Maiwand and had shown great gallantry. I stood in front of the house, with my back to the portico, a Sergeant with the colours next to me, and 200 of the 66th Regt. (now called Berkshire, with white facings, instead of green) under the command of Col. Hogge, were formed up in a square, facing me. They had their little dog, a sort of Pomeranian with them, which had been with them through the campaign and is devoted to the men. It disappeared after Maiwand, but came back with Sir F. Roberts, when he entered Kandahar, and instantly recognised the remaining men of the Regt. "Bobby" as he is called, is a great pet and had a velvet coat on, embroidered with pearls and two good conduct stripes and other devices and orders tied round its neck. It was wounded in the back but had quite recovered.*

Victoria had found her first Pom within seven years after awarding that regiment in India good conduct medals, and Poms remained with her for the rest of her life. Just before she succumbed to a final illness in January 1901, her deathbed wish was to have her little pet Pom, Turi, at her side. This was done and the little dog laid down on the bed beside his dying mistress.

---

*Reprinted with the gracious permission of Her Majesty the Queen.

This unsigned painting of a white Pomeranian (circa 1880) with a blue ribbon tied around its neck exemplifies "my lady's pet." From the collection of Richard Hammond.   *Fox & Cook*

H.A. Crowther painted this 1916 orange with cream shading Pomeranian, which shows the heavier features of the larger early English Pom. From the collection of Richard Hammond.

Fox & Cook

4

English Pomeranians

ENGLAND'S FIRST OFFICIAL organized dog show
took place in the Town Hall of Newcastle-upon-Tyne on June 28
and 29, 1859 and featured just Pointers and Setters. The first all-
breed show was held the following year at Cheapside in Birming-
ham. It was not until 1870 that the smallish Spitz-type dog was
formally recognized by the English Kennel Club under the name
Pomeranian. Individual classes were permitted for the acknowl-
edged breed in 1871, where one show recorded an entry of three of
the larger white specimens. The broad attention to the Poms did not
begin, however, until after Queen Victoria's celebrated ownership of
the animals. While in 1890 not a single Pom was entered in an
English dog show, 1905 saw 125 shown at a single event.

As the above figures demonstrate, acceptance by exhibitors and
serious breeders of the Pomeranian dog was slow in coming.
Stonehenge recounts in 1872:

> This cheerful little dog is extremely common on the Continent of
> Europe, where it goes by the name of Loup-Loup. Until lately it was
> very rare in England, but within the last twenty years it has become

very common as a house-dog. It is not recognized, however, by the fanciers, and is not highly prized by anybody, being of no use but as a companion. The head is very fox-like, with pricked ears and a sharp nose; neck thick, and covered with a ruff of woolly hair; body also clothed with thick woolly hair; not curled; legs free from hair. Tail carried high, and curled over the back, but not so closely as that of the pure Pug Dog. Color generally white, sometimes a pale-cream color, and more rarely black.

Lillian C. Raymond-Mallock, an English breeder of Pekingese, expanded on Stonehenge's opinion, writing in 1910:

The first dogs we hear of were of a pale yellow color; they were rather long in body, but very fox-like in head, expression, and movement, and they eventually became extinct. The Spitz made his debut on our show bench as a pure white animal, though the tinge of yellow about the ears of a white specimen (which is now counted a grave fault) leads to the impression that in all probability he was descended from the old yellow variety. Later on, black and other coloured dogs were imported from Germany. They were much smaller than our own white ones, and so began the breeding of toy Poms.

Early Breed Standards

Size became the governing factor for the English Pom breeders of the late 1890s, as the breed gradually gained acceptance. A group of breeders met during the Cruft's show in February 1891 for the purpose of forming a club. Called the Pomeranian Club of England, one of its first priorities was to establish a breed standard, which underwent several revisions before being finally accepted. This is one of the earliest versions:

Appearance—The Pomeranian should be compact, short coupled dog, well knit in frame. He should exhibit great intelligence in his expression, and activity and buoyancy in his deportment. **Head and Nose**—Should be foxy in outline or wedge-shaped, the skull being slightly flat, large in proportion to the muzzle, which should finish rather flat and free from lippiness. The teeth should be level, and should on no account be undershot. The hair on the head and face should be smooth and short-coated. The nose should be black in white, orange and sable dogs; but in other colours may be self, but

This modern English-bred Pomeranian, Ch. Rosskear's Triple Echo, is the holder of the English breed record with 34 challenge certificates. Owned and bred by Anne R. Winter of Rosskear Kennels, South Wales.

R. Willbie

English Ch. Derronill's Maxamillion was the Supreme Best Toy at Crufts in 1986. Owned and bred by Derek Hill. *Fall*

never parti-coloured or white. **Ears**—Should be small, not set too far apart, nor too low down, but carried perfectly erect like those of a fox, and, like the head, should be covered with short, soft hair. **Eyes**— Should be medium in size, not full, nor set too wide apart, bright and dark in colour, showing great intelligence; in white, shaded sable, or orange dogs the rims round the eyes should be black. **Neck and Body**—The neck should be rather short, well set in. The back must be short and the body compact, being well ribbed up and the barrel well rounded. The chest must be fairly deep and not too wide, but in proportion to the size of the dog. **Legs**—The fore-legs must be well feathered, perfectly straight, of medium length, and not such as would be termed "leggy" or "low" on leg, but in proportion in length and strength to a well-balanced frame. Must be fine in bone and free in action. The hind-legs and thighs must be well feathered, neither contracted nor wide behind; the feet small and compact in shape. Shoulders should be clean, and well laid back. **Tail**—The tail is one of the characteristics of the breed, and should be turned over the back and carried flat and straight, being profusely covered with long, harsh, spreading hair. **Coat**—There should be two coats, an undercoat and an overcoat; the one a soft fluffy undercoat, the other a long, perfectly straight coat, harsh in texture, covering the whole of the body, being very abundant round the neck and fore part of the shoulders and chest where it should form a frill of profuse standing off straight hair, extending over the shoulders. The hind-quarters should be clad with long hair or feathering, from the top of the rump to the hock. **Colour**—All whole colours are admissible, but they should be free from white or shadings, and the whites must be quite free from lemon or any other colour. A few white hairs in any of the self colours shall not necessarily disqualify. At present the whole coloured dogs are: white, black, brown (light or dark), blue (as pale as possible), orange (which should be deep and even in colour as possible), beaver, or cream. Dogs, other than white, with white foot or feet, leg or legs, are decidedly objectionable and should be discouraged, and cannot compete as whole coloured specimens. In parti-coloured dogs the colours should be evenly distributed on the body in patches; a dog with white or tan feet or chest would not be a parti-colour. Shaded sables should be shaded throughout with three or more colours, the hairs to be as "uniformly shaded" as possible, with no patches of self colour. In mixed classes where whole coloured and parti-coloured Pomeranians compete together, the preference should, if on other points they are equal, be given to the whole coloured specimens. Where classification is not by colours the following is recommended

Ch. Hadleigh Shining Star, owned and bred by
Mrs. Gladys Dyke, was England's top-winning
Pom until 1986.   *Sally Anne Thompson*

rs. Gladys Dyke's Hadleigh Kennels is one of England's premier Pomeranian kennels. Mrs. Dyke
urchased her first Pom in 1938 and to date her dogs have won approximately 500 challenge
rtificates and acquired nearly 100 English championships. Ch. Hadleigh Twinkling Star is a typical
adleigh dog.   *Sally Anne Thompson*

for adoption by show committees: 1. Not exceeding 7 lb. (Pomeranian Miniatures). 2. Exceeding 7 lbs. (Pomeranians). 3. Pomeranians and Pomeranian Miniatures mixed.

The early English Pomeranian weighed from 10 to 12 pounds up to 20 pounds or more, but the breeders quickly moved to breed smaller dogs. Indeed Miss Lillian Ives wrote that during standard discussions the question about proper weight became "a sore point." As she recalls in her book *Show Pomeranians* (1929):

Endless discussions took place, for neither individual members nor individual clubs (for here I should point out that with the growth in popularity of the breed in all parts of the country, had sprung up district Pomeranian Clubs in the North of England, Scotland, Midlands, Ireland, etc.) seemed absolutely in accord as to the division of weight most desirable. Popular fancy turned to small dogs, and 5 lbs. was suggested as a suitable division, only to be rejected. There were not many heavyweights, but beautiful dogs of between six and eight pounds were meeting with little encouragement, however typical they might be, or however great their value as stud dogs, the prizes being mostly annexed by the more diminutive specimens. The majority of the members of the different clubs finally came into accord, and submitted the matter to the Kennel Club, the result being that the divisional weight was altered to 7 lb. instead of 8 lb. This more rational division retained the most useful dogs in the list, both as show dogs and sires, while not excluding the smaller specimens, which continued to hold sway on the show bench-dogs of from 4 to 5½ lb. Dogs of this weight and smaller are now the more popular, but at the weight named they are the most reliable and useful stud dogs and brood bitches.

Several authorities of the day expressed the thought that the breed would not have continued in Britain if it had not been for two main motivations: (1) the desire and ability to successfully breed down in size the original 20 to 30 lb. dog without damaging the health of the animal, and (2) the variety of colors that were easily obtainable and subsequently popular. The smaller size, delightful coat and lovely colors made the Pom a fashionable dog to own. Of all the colors, a sable Pom was regarded as "canine chic." The

Ch. Sweet Lady of Hadleigh, owned and bred by
Mrs. Gladys Dyke.   *Fall*

Hadleigh Dancing Master is considered by some
as one of the best coated Pomeranians ever.
Matsuno

Ch. Hadleigh Honey Puff won 31 challenge
certificates before her retirement.
Sally Anne Thompson

Ch. Rosskear Winterwonderland, owned and bred by Anne Winter.   *Pearce*

Anne Winter of Rosskear Kennels in South Wales has been breeding Pomeranians since 1972. Ten of her British champions have won 116 challenge certificates. Ch. Wynwrights Mid-Winter Boy is one of her champions.
Pearce

Ch. Ringland's Gaiety Girl at Rosskear.

breed's new development and consequential fame quickly spread from England across the Atlantic Ocean to America.

Today's English Pomeranians are considered by many fanciers as being some of the finest specimens in the world. Their compact bodies, harsh stand-offish coats and beautiful heads are sought after by breeders everywhere.

Ch. Derronill's Desire is an English bitch bred by Derek Hill, chairman of England's national breed club, the Pomeranian Club. Desire is owned by Derek Hill and Carl Sparrow. *Dave Freeman*

One of the earliest successful Pom breeders was Mrs. Vincent Matta, shown here with Ch. Dixieland's Shining Gold—a prominent figure in many pedigrees.

One of Ch. Dixieland's Shining Gold's sons was Ch. Little Timstopper, first owned by Mrs. Matta and later sold to Mrs. James M. Austin. Among Timstopper's many wins was top group honors in 1947 at both the Westminster and Morris and Essex shows.

5

American Pomeranians

THE EVOLUTION OF the Pomeranian breed in America closely paralleled that of its mother country, Great Britain. Many early American dogs were imported from England and initially were of the larger white variety.

Breed Beginnings in America

In 1888, the American Kennel Club entered the first Pomeranian in its stud book. The dog was simply called "Dick" and given number 10776. Shown originally in the Miscellaneous Class—a potpourri of breeds with no official class designation—the Pom was usually referred to as a Spitz.

It has been surmised that a dog known as "Sheffield Lad" was the first documented Pomeranian-type dog shown in the United States at a New York show in 1892. There are no further accounts until 1896 when two Poms, Prince Bismarck and Wolfgang, won second and third, respectively, in the Miscellaneous Class in New York. Pomeranians continued to be spottedly shown for the next few years, and it was not until 1900 that the breed received individual class designation and was officially recognized by the American Kennel Club.

This was also the time that a group of American fanciers joined together to form the American Pomeranian Club. Following in England's footsteps, the breeders began emphasizing size reduction and acceptance of various colors. Swiftly the breed gained in popularity among the ladies and gentlemen of the day.

The 1900 American standard was:

Appearance—The Pomeranian in build and appearance should be of a compact, short-coupled dog, well knit in frame. His head and face should be fox-like, with small, erect ears that appear to be sensible to every sound. He should exhibit great intelligence in his expression, docility in his disposition, and activity and buoyancy in his deportment.

Head—The head should be somewhat foxy in outline, or wedge-shaped, the skull being slightly flat (although in the toy varieties the skull may be rather rounder), large in proportion to the muzzle, which should finish rather fine and be free from lippiness. The teeth should be level and on no account undershot. The head in its profile may exhibit a little stop, which, however, must not be too pronounced, and the hair on the head and face must be smooth or short-coated.

Eyes—The eyes should be medium size, rather oblique in shape, not set too wide apart, bright and dark in colour, showing great intelligence and docility of temper. In the white dog black rims around the eyes are preferable.

Ears—The ears should be small, not set too wide apart nor too low down, and carried perfectly erect, like those of a fox, and like the head should be covered with soft short hair. No plucking or trimming is allowable.

Nose—In black, black and tan or white dogs the nose should be black; in other coloured Pomeranians it may often be brown or liver-coloured, but in all cases the nose must be self- not parti-coloured, and never white.

Neck and Shoulders—The neck if anything should be rather short, well set in and lion-like covered with a profuse mane and frill of long straight hair, sweeping from the under jaw and covering the whole of the front part of the shoulders and chest, as well as the top part of the shoulders. The shoulders must be tolerably clean and laid well back.

Body—The back must be short, and the body compact, being well ribbed up and barrel well rounded. The chest must be fairly deep and not too wide.

Legs—The fore legs must be perfectly straight, of medium length, not such as would be termed either "leggy" or "low on the leg," but in due proportion in length and strength to a well balanced frame, and the fore legs and thighs must be well feathered, the feet small and compact in shape. No trimming is allowable.

Tail—The tail is characteristic of the breed, and should be turned over the back and carried flat, being profusely covered with long spreading hair.

Coat—Properly speaking there should be two coats—an under and over coat; the one a soft fluffy undercoat, and the other a long, perfectly straight and glistening coat, covering the whole of the body, being very abundant round the neck and fore part of the shoulders and chest, where it should form a frill of profuse standing-off straight hair, extending over the shoulders as previously described. The hindquarters, like those of the collie, should be similarly clad with long hair or feathering from the top of the rump to the hocks. The hair on the tail must be, as previously stated, profuse and spreading over the back.

Colour—The following colours are admissible: white, black, blue or grey, brown, sable or shaded sable (including red, orange or fawn), and parti-colours. The whites must be quite free from lemon or any colour, and the blacks, blues, browns and sables from any white. A few white hairs on any of the self-colours shall not absolutely disqualify, but should carry great weight against a dog. In parti-coloured dogs the colours should be evenly distributed on the body in patches; a dog with a white foot or a white chest would not be a parti-coloured. Whole-coloured dogs with a white foot or feet, leg or legs, are decidedly objectionable, and should be discouraged, and cannot compete as whole-coloured specimens. In mixed classes, where whole-coloured and parti-coloured compete together, the preference should be given to the whole-coloured specimens, if in other points they are equal.

Weight—Where classification by weight is made, the following scale should be adopted by show committees: 1. Not exceeding eight pounds. 2. Exceeding eight pounds.

Colour Classification—Where classification by colour is made, the following should be adopted: 1. Black. 2. White. 3. Brown or chocolate. 4. Sable and shaded sable. 5. Blue or grey. 6. Any other colour.

Ch. Gold Mist of Waverly, an early Best in Show winning bitch, was owned and shown by Anna LaFortune, Sungold Kennels.

Ch. Aristic Dear Adorable was a multi-group and BIS winning Pomeranian bitch, owned and shown by Mary S. Brewster and bred by Gladys Schoenberg, Aristic Kennels. Dear Adorable was a great, great granddaughter of Ch. Dixieland's Shining Gold.

Tauskey

SCALE OF POINTS

Appearance	15	Body	10
Head	5	Legs	5
Eyes	5	Tail	10
Ears	5	Coat	25
Nose	5	Colour	10
Neck and Shoulders	5		
Total			100

In any attempt to compare this early standard with that of Great Britain, previously quoted herein, it is necessary to remember that both countries were experimenting with qualifying descriptive perfections for the breed. Britain had already changed "glistening coat" to a clearer "harsh coat," while the United States had added mention about the need for a "stop" and specifically permitted black rims around the eyes of white dogs. Also the English standard had not yet included sable descriptions under color, as sables were just coming into acceptance when that edition of the standard was written.

Further Breed Development

The American Pomeranian Club became a member club of the American Kennel Club in 1909 and held its first specialty show in 1911. This event was judged by Mrs. L. C. Dyer from England and drew an entry of 138 dogs. The second annual specialty show was judged by American authority, Charles G. Hopton, and drew 185 entries.

During the infant years of organized and AKC-recognized dog shows, all breeds—other than the miscellaneous—were categorized into one of two groups: the Sporting Group and the Non-Sporting Group. After graduating from the Miscellaneous Class into their own classification, the Pomeranian breed was placed in the Non-Sporting Group. It was not until March 1928 that the American Kennel Club splintered the two groups into five variety groups. Those groups were the Sporting, Hound, Terrier, Toy and Non-

Sporting. The Pomeranian was then re-categorized into the Toy Group, where it remains to this day.

An AKC *Gazette* article of May 31, 1924, entitled "What an Old Virtue Has Done" and written under the pseudonym Pomerania, describes the development of the Pom in America:

> If the World War did nothing else, it certainly helped the dog industry of the United States. Prior to 1914 it was the custom for the American Fancy to go to England for its best blood of more than one important breed. When the great war forced breeding to be stopped in England, the dog lovers of this country discovered that excellent animals could be bred here, and today England is no longer the "mother country" of our dogs.
>
> The statement is particularly true of the Pomeranian. There was a time when Americans naturally turned to England for this handsome little Toy. There is no questioning the hard fact that Americans should feel grateful to English breeders for their start. But patience has rewarded the American fanciers. During the past few years, many grand Pomeranians have been produced in the United States. Today, the American Fancy no longer has to depend upon England for her show specimens or breeding stock.
>
> It is an interesting fact that English judges have acknowledged the statement that American-bred Pomeranians are now equal to those that are bred in the British Isles. They have been kind enough to congratulate American breeders, a congratulation that is well deserved. The American-bred animal is gaining in every point. American breeders and fanciers have cultivated patience, and by so doing have likewise cultivated good stock.
>
> Experience has taught the lovers of all dogs that it requires from three to four generations to correct faulty breeding. This great truth has recently been absorbed by the Pomeranian fancy. Formerly they saw only pedigrees. Today the American breeders of this little dog can point with pride to the animals that have been raised in the United States.
>
> Experience is always costly. American Pomeranian fanciers have paid dearly for their experience. But it has been well worth buying. Today it is no uncommon thing to see an American bred placed over an imported Pom. As a result, the market for foreign stock in the United States is not as good as it was in former years. Interest in the home-bred never wanes, and a breeder is spurred on by defeat to attempt to do better and more glorious things.

Ch. Lennis's Tar Lacy
Foxfire, bred by Wanda
Paxton, owned by
Edward B. Jenner and
shown by Susan Heckman
Buckel, won the Toy
Group at Westminster in
1979.
Ashbey

Ch. Great Elms Prince Charming II, bred by Ruth Beam and owned by Olga Baker and Skip Piazza, comes from a long line of top-winning Great Elms Pomeranians. *Kernan*

Ch. D'Nee's Darin Duffie, bred and owned by Nadine Hersil, was shown to many Group 1s and BISs by Jacqueline Liddle. *Missy*

44

Ch. Bonner's Peppersweet Red Pod.

Shafer

Dorothy Bonner is another long-time Pomeranian breeder. She showed Ch. Bonner's Stylepepper Preshus to Best in Show at the Pom's first dog show.

Ch. Ardencaple's Mightly Might, an early 1960s winner, owned by Mr. and Mrs. Willard K. Denton and shown by Frank Ashbey.

Shafer

Ch. T Town Serenade, bred by T Town Kennels
and owned by Lady Florence Conyers.

Brown

Ch. Pixietown Serenade of Hadleigh did a lot of winning in the early 1960s. Here he sits
in the Westminster Kennel Club's Toy Group winner silver bowl that he won in 1962.
Co-owned by Lady Florence Conyers and Ruth Bellick, he was shown by Winifred
Heckman.   *Shafer*

Ch. Edward's Reddy Career, owned by Mary S.
and Joy S. Brewster, Robwood Kennels, and bred
by Edd E. Bivin. *Brown*

Ch. Hadleigh Shining Gold of Davdon, a British import and American group and BIS
winner, shown by Joy S. Brewster and owned by Robwood Kennels, wins a 1956 Toy
Group under judge Isodore Schoenberg. Isodore and Gladys Schoenberg formed the
famed Aristic Kennels in Texas. *Shafer*

There is no more exquisite toy than the Pomeranian. It is truly a toy dog. The breed is a fixture and will continue so until the end of time. Also, Pomeranians never will become common, as they are not prolific. Of course, there are color fashions in these little animals. At the present time, the breeders are going in strongly for blacks, and black matrons are in great demand.

The orange-sable Pomeranian is here to stay. They are showing the true graduated colors. While there are not many orange Poms in this country, the ones seen are lovely in color. Incidentally, their number is increasing with every show.

The beautiful silver-wolf sable also is coming to the fore. The rusty wolf seems to have disappeared, the clear chinchilla taking its place. While few creams are bred, those showing are good and are free from lemon tints.

As the American Pomeranian fancy now has stock "par excellence," it is to be hoped that it will choose carefully, breed carefully and keep color line within bounds. The habit of breeding chocolates to oranges should be discouraged. Our sables, oranges, black and chocolates have their proper mates. All are good ones. If the American breeder will continue to cultivate the habit of patience, good stock is bound to follow.*

Good stock has followed. In the past 60 plus years since that article appeared in the *Gazette* the Pomerian breed in America has definitely flourished. 17,908 Pomeranian litters were registered by the American Kennel Club in 1986, with 25,056 individual Poms being registered during the same year. The little Poms have captured many Best in Show prizes at some of the top shows in the country and their popularity as a pet and show dog continues to be strong. Quality breeders find their lines readily sought throughout the world.

---

*Reprinted with the permission of the American Kennel Club.

6

German and Dutch Pomeranians

IN GERMANY, which is often considered the country of origin for the Pomeranian, the northern Spitz, or what the Germans refer to as the "Torf" group of dogs, has existed for thousands of years. Archaeologists have discovered skeleton remains of prehistoric dogs of this group at Bodensee, Lake Constance and some Swiss lakes.

Not only were Pomeranians favorite dogs of royal families, they were also highly prized pets of successful composers, artists, scientists and theologians. Mrs. Eyke Schmidt-Rohde of West Germany says:

> Such a breed can look back on a long tradition of being of service to mankind. There were many prominent people who were Pomeranian lovers: the reformer Martin Luther mentioned his beloved Pomeranian "Belferlein" in numerous theological writings; Michelangelo was also escorted by his Pomeranian. Lying on a satin pillow, the dog watched his master paint the ceiling of the Sistine Chapel; Isaac

Newton, the famous physicist and astronomer, had his manuscripts torn up by his Pomeranian, "Diamond"; Mozart dedicated a little aria to "Pimperl," his female Pomeranian; and Chopin was so stimulated by the lively games of his girlfriend's Pomeranian that he composed the "Valse des Petits Chiens" for the little dog.

German Classifications

Germans regard their Pomeranians to be a variety within a larger German Spitz classification. There are five Spitz categories:

Wolfsspitz (Great or Keeshond). Color: wolf-grey, silver grey with touch of black on hairtips. Height: 45–60 cm. at withers.

Grobspitz (German Giant or Great Spitz). Color: white, black, brown. Height: 40–50 cm. at withers.

Mittelspitz (Middle Spitz). Color: black, white, brown, orange, wolf-grey. Height: 29–36 cm. at withers.

Kleinspitz (Small Spitz). Color: black, white, brown, orange, wolf-sable. Height: 23–28 cm. at withers; corresponds with the larger Poms found in America or England.

Zwergspitz (Dwarf Spitz). Color: all colors permitted. Height: not more than 22 cm. at withers; corresponds with the smaller Poms found in America or England.

The Verein Fue Deutsche Spitze E.V. (German Spitz and Pomeranian Club, also known as German Association of Pomeranians, Reg.) was founded in 1899 and is the parent club that oversees all the Spitz varieties. In Germany, the kennel clubs and dog shows function under the auspices of the Federation Cynoloqique Internationale (FCI) and the adopted breed standards are the FCI standards used by all FCI show-giving countries. A translation of the present FCI standard for the Kleinspitz and Zwergspitz appears in the appendix.

The Germans are very color and size conscious and maintain careful breeding standards. They like a different type of Pom than that which is usually seen in America or England. The German Pom tends to be slightly heavier in bone, with a more distinctive "foxy" expression and a longer muzzle and ears.

50

A trio of dark chocolate Kleinspitz brood bitches, owned by Mrs. Waltraud Omlin, West Germany.

Betty Edelweiss vom Hans Gohfeld, World Champion white Kleinspitz, owned by Karl Busse, West Germany.

This Dutch puppy, owned and
bred by Mrs. Saes-Vaessen,
Holland, is an English-type Pom.

A group-winning Dutch Pom bitch, Bumble Bee van het Pinneland, owned and bred by
Mrs. Saes-Vaessen, Holland.

Dutch Classifications

Pomeranians in Holland also are categorized with other Spitz varieties and come under the general heading of the Keeshonden. The *Nederlandse Keeshonden Club* (Dutch Keeshond Club) was founded in 1924 to encompass all these Spitz or Keeshonden varieties. Today the five sizes are divided as Wolfgrey Keeshond; White, black and brown Keeshonden; *Middlenslag Keeshonden; Klein Keeshonden;* and *Dwergkeeshonden.* The Kleine Keeshond and Dwergkeeshond represent the smaller types. Ms. Carry Saes, a second-generation Pomeranian breeder and judge, offers some insights on the status of Poms in Holland:

> In Germany, people do not like the Poms with the shorter muzzles. They want them fox-like and this sometimes results in Poms with long ears and long, snipy muzzles. In Holland, the situation is different. We are somewhere in the middle between German and English opinion. We have, of course, to stick to the German standard, but prefer the English type of Pom. We have good orange Poms. We also have some nice blacks. Whites are more difficult as there are not many to choose from.

Holland breeders benefit from being close to both England and Germany. Although they do not show their dogs in England due to the quarantine restrictions, they can easily import breeding stock. They seem to prefer the orange color, which is probably due to the imported English strains.

The German breeders, on the other hand, prefer to stress strict color standards. They greatly favor chocolate, black and white dogs. Mrs. Schmidt-Rohde reports that black Poms are preferred in southern Germany, especially in the Wurttemberg area, while whites are favored in northern Germany. The wolfgrey dogs are generally found along the Rhine River. These areas of color distinctions closely follow those of over 200 years ago when Queen Charlotte, who came from northern Germany, brought white "Pommeranians" with her to England, and Queen Victoria's Marco, although found in Italy, was bred in southern Germany. The present day Pomeranians tend to be smaller or, if larger, classified in a different variety. Nevertheless, color remains important in the breeder's mind.

A head study of a white Pomeranian with the required black points. Brooker's Rumblin Tumble Weed, owned by Sophie Mayes, had two white parents.

This black Pom, Ch. May Morning Hokus Pokus, double black bred, was owned by Sophie Mayes, May Morning Kennel.

7

Colors

THE PRESENT OFFICIAL American standard for
the Pomeranian (approved October 14, 1980) states the following
under "color":

Acceptable colors to be judged on a equal basis; any solid color, any
solid color with lighter or darker shadings of the same color, any solid
color with sable or black shadings, parti-color, sable and black &
tan. . . .

As we have read, in the early standards of England and the
United States not all colors were equally presented or accepted when
the Pomeranian became formally recognized as an individual breed
in those countries.

The original British Poms favored by the nobility and upper
classes during the 1750s had been imported from the northern
provinces of Germany and were white in color. Later, black Poms
from southern Germany became popular. These were subsequently
followed by browns, shaded sables, creams, blues, beavers, reds,
oranges and parti-colors. Although almost all colors were acceptable, steps had been taken to favor solid and whole colors and the

World Ch. Maja von Tannenhof, a dark chocolate Kleinspitz.

On the left is World Ch. Viko vom Tannenhof, who is black; beside him is his chocolate colored daughter, World Ch. Maja vom Tannenhof. Both dogs are bred and owned by Mrs. Waltraud Omlin, West Germany.

standards reflected that stance—hence the statement, "In mixed classes where whole coloured and parti-coloured Pomeranians compete together, the preference should be given to the whole-coloured specimens, if in other points they are equal."

Up until 15 years ago, the American standard defined the permissible breed colors thusly:

Twelve colors, or color combinations, are permissible and recognized, namely, black, brown, chocolate, beaver, red, orange, cream, orange-sable, wolf-sable, blue, white, and parti-color. The beaver color is a dark beige. A parti-color is white with orange or black color distributed in even patches on the body, with white blaze on head desirable. Where whole-colored and parti-colored Pomeranians compete together, the preference should, other points being equal, be given to the whole-colored specimen. Sable-colored dogs must be shaded throughout as uniformly as possible, with no self-colored patches. In orange-sable, the undercoat must be a light tan with deeper orange guard hairs ending in black tippings. In wolf-sable, the undercoat is light gray with a deeper shade of steel-gray guard hairs ending in black tippings. A shaded muzzle on the sables is permissible, but a black mask on sables is a minor fault. Orange Pomeranians must be self-colored throughout, with light shadings of the same tone (not white) breechings permitted. A black mask on an orange Pomeranian is a minor fault. White chest, white foot, or white leg on whole-colored dogs are major faults. White hairs on black, brown, blue or sable Pomeranians are objectionable. Tinges of lemon or any other color on white dogs are objectionable. The above colors, as described, are the only allowable colors or combination of colors for Pomeranians.

In March 1971, the standard regarding color restrictions was totally revised due to pressure from breeders who wanted all colors to be permissible:

Acceptable colors to be judged on an equal basis; any solid color, any solid color with lighter or darker shadings of the same color, any solid color with sable or black shadings, parti-color, sable and black & tan. Black & tan is black with tan or rust, sharply defined, appearing above each eye and on muzzle, throat, and forechest, on all legs and feet and below the tail. Parti-color is white with any other color distributed in even patches on the body and a white blaze on head.

57

In 1980, a further sentence was added to this section of the American standard:

A white chest, foot, or leg on a whole-colored dog (except white) is a major fault.

This sentence merely served to correct the omission of a single white spot on whole-colored dogs as a major fault from the 1971 revision.

Color Definitions

Some present day color definitions are:

White. The earliest popular Pomeranians had been white in color. Unfortunately, they had also been rather large with narrow heads, long muzzles and large ears. When the smaller dogs came into vogue, breeders who emphasized the white color tried to breed their animals down in size by mating with smaller dogs who happened to be of other colors. The result was usually parti-colors or wolf sables. Those who were successful in maintaining a white strain of smaller Poms often produced dogs that had a soft, short coat. Some had difficulties keeping the desired dark pigment or points. Others lost the solid white color with the appearance of lemon patches and tippings. Today it is difficult to breed a quality, true white colored typey dog with the desired black points—nose, eye rims, lips and foot pads. Almost all whites are born snow-white with pink points. As the puppy ages, the points will darken, but the coat will remain pure white.

Cream. Cream has been described as a variation of white—a very pale liver or yellow color. Breeders have reported that a cream is a "sport," or genetic surprise, that can come from black, white, shaded sables or oranges. Cream is sometimes referred to as a very light orange, but many breeders regard this as a misnomer. A cream is an even self-color throughout with no white breechings or underparts. Due to the harsher texture of the guard hairs, the top coat may appear slightly deeper in color than the undercoat. Creams must have black points.

Black. The black Pomeranian was extremely popular in the breed's early years, but its popularity declined when shaded sables came into existence and many good black bitches were taken from legitimate strains and mated to other colors in an effort to produce sables. Several current breeders are trying to revitalize the solid black Pom without losing the essence of breed type. A black is generally pictured as pure "coal black," completely devoid of any white, red or brown hairs. The coat is usually profuse and has good texture.

Brown. The color brown includes all shades from the deepest, darkest chocolate to the lighter beaver. The chocolate is a rich dark chocolate candy color that is self-colored throughout. A brown is more a milk chocolate, occasionally appearing with lighter shadings, and the beaver has been referred to as a dark beige. Beavers are seldom seen today. Browns and chocolates are more prevalent on the European continent than the United States. In all cases, the dogs need to be kept out of the sun as the coat color will fade in sunlight and carry a reddish tinge. The nose, eye rims, lips and foot pads are acceptable in brown, and are occasionally so dark that they appear to be black.

Blue. Blue is a color that is seldom seen today, yet at one time it had been highly favored. The slate or silvery color is extremely difficult to breed as the color breeds true: a blue must be bred to a blue to guarantee blue offspring. Occasionally one might get a blue from black, brown or sable dogs, but this is a recessive throwback that is unreliable for color breeding. Breeders who have tried to establish blue strains recommend selecting the best throwbacks from several generations for matings. Occasional outcrossings with cream or white are recommended for lightening and improving the clarity of the blue color. Blue puppies are born the color of new silver or black before developing a silvery gray undercoat and a darker slate blue top coat with dark blue nose, eye rims, lips and foot pads.

Orange. Currently one of the most popular colors, a proper orange-colored coat is a bright, clear orange that varies from a light orange to a deep, rich orange. Occasionally there are light shadings on the breeches and bibs. Dark shadings would make the animal an orange-sable. Sometimes breeders cross a pure orange with an orange-sable to both brighten the orange coat and prevent the sable from darkening too much. A "blonde" is considered not a cream, but a very light orange with or without lighter and possibly white shadings.

Red. A true red is not a dark orange, but a deep, rusty clear red.

Shaded Sables. Shaded sables are dogs whose coats are shaded throughout with three or more colors. This shading must be as uniform as possible with no patches of self-color. Sables generally have the best texture and length of all the coat colors. An orange-sable has a light orange or creamy undercoat with deeper orange guard hairs ending in black tippings. In red-sables the base colors have red hues with black tippings. Cream-sables possess cream variations with black tippings. A wolf-sable has a light gray undercoat with a deeper shade of steel gray guard hairs ending in black tippings. Unless reversed, there must be no cream or orange cast to the base color. A reverse sable is where the colors are reversed.

Parti-Color. A parti-color Pomerian is a dog with more than one coat color. The colors are evenly distributed in even patches on the body. A white blaze on the head is required in the present U.S. breed standard. A white chest, foot or leg on an otherwise solid color or sable does not constitute a parti-color. Such marking is a major breed fault. Parti-colors are one of the original color combinations for the Pomeranians and are considered sports from matings between whites, blacks, blues and shaded sables. Early parti-colors had often been overweight or large sized, and in the quest for the smaller dog they declined in popularity. Several American breeders are presently striving to produce quality parti-colored Pomeranians with the necessary black points.

Black & Tan. Black & tans are black Poms with tan or rust, sharply defined, appearing above each eye and on both sides of the muzzle, on the throat and forechest, on all legs and feet and just below the tail. Black & tans are not parti-colors. Since black is the base color, the dogs should have a black nose, eye rims and lips.

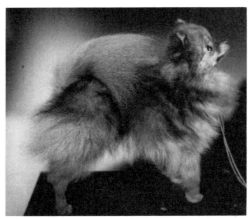

Eng. and Am. Ch. Solitaire of Morrell and Robwood, an English import owned by Mary S. Brewster, was a dark orange shaded sable.

Sable shadings on a lighter orange can be seen in this "through the looking glass" portrait by ʰn Ashbey of Ch. Lennis's Tar Lacy Foxfire, owned by Ed Jenner.   *Ashbey*

Ch. Silva Lade Christmas Joy, a black & tan bitch, owned and bred by Dianne Johnson.
Cott/Daigle

Ch. Prestigious Pee Wee Parti, a parti-color owned by Sherry and Earl Steinmetz and bred by Dorothy West.   *Olson*

Am. and Can. Ch. Jabil's Dandilion, CD, was a lovely bright clear orange. Bred and owned by Jessie and Barbara Young, Jabil Kennels.

8

The Genetics of Pomeranian Color

As WE KNOW, Pomeranians exist in a variety of coat colors. How are these colors attained? What is their genetic makeup? C. William Ledbetter, an American presently residing in West Germany, prepared the following study of Pomeranian color genetics.

The Forms of Gene A

A^s allows a distribution of dark pigment over the whole body surface (dominant, this gene is inherited from at least one parent in a black Pomeranian)

a^y restricts the areas of dark hair pigment and produces usually a clear sable; a weakened form of this gene can produce various dilutions of red, orange or even cream, with or without sable

a^t produces bicolor black-and-tan or chocolate-and-tan

Pomeranians; this gene can be covered up by the gene A^s or extremely modified by the gene a^y to resemble sable

a^w produces the gray of wolf-sable (can be covered up by A^s; can be covered up or extremely modified by either the presence of a^y or a^t)

The forms of Gene B

B produces black pigmentation of nose, footpads and eye rims; produces black pigment granules in both the inner and outer layers of each hair strand

b produces brown or chocolate pigmentation of nose and eye rims; restricts the pigment formation in the hair to chocolate or lighter reddish-brown shades

The Forms of Gene C

C the gene for full depth of pigmentation; produces a deep, rich *intensity* of orange, red, chocolate or black hair coloring

c^{ch} the gene for chinchilla-coloring; greatly reduces the red-yellow pigment of the hair, leaving the black pigment; found in the true wolf-sable Pomeranians in accompaniment with the gene a^w; commonly found in dog breeds such as the Norwegian Elkhound

c^w this gene is found in pure-white German Spitz and Pomeranians. It reduces all pigmentation of the hair to white, leaving the pigmentation of eyes, nose, eye rims and foot-pads either black or brown.
Not completely recessive, this gene can weaken the effect of gene C, so that Poms of mixed red/white or orange/white breeding become dilute orange or cream in coat color. Blacks of mixed black/white breeding may have white feet or toes.

c^a produces complete albinism, dogs with a white coat and pink eyes; very rare in Pomeranians

The Forms of Gene D

D   regulates a heavy deposit of all pigment granules in each hair strand

d   dilutes the black pigmentation, as in true blues (for example, the blue Maltese), or the dilute chocolate pigmentation as seen in beaver-colored dogs (for example, Weimaraners) is produced by this gene

The Forms of Gene E

E   allows the formation of black or chocolate pigment in each hair strand

e   permits *no* formation of dark (black or chocolate) pigment in the hair, but does *not* influence red or yellow pigment (certain types of orange Pomeranians and certain types of "Irish Setter red" Pomeranians can have this gene, along with the gene A^s; when mated with an orange or red with or without sable but with the gene E, black pups may be the product

E^m produces a black mask

e^{br} produces brindle in combination with a^y or a^t

The Forms of Gene G

G   changes a puppy, which is at birth of a uniformly *dark* color, later in the direction of increasing grayness or pale shading

g   constant pigmentation

The Forms of Gene M

m   uniform pigmentation

produces merle (dapple) coats, often with areas of white; often one or both eyes are light blue or have blotchy (variegated) iris pigmentation

The Forms of Gene P

P normal pigment formation

p reduces black pigmentation to "lilac" and chocolate to light yellowish fawn

The Forms of Gene S

S solid-colored coat with no white or very minute spots of white on toes and chest

s^p parti-colored Pomeranians

The Forms of Gene T

T flecks or "ticking" in white areas of the coat

t clear-white, unticked coat

Using the above symbols and the symbol x for any other gene form of the letter to the left of the symbol x, Pomeranians in the various colors will have the following genetic makeups:

Black:

A^sx   Bx   Cx   Dx   Ex   Sx   gg   mm   Px   tt

Chocolate-colored:

A^sx   bb   Cx   Dx   Ex   Sx   gg   mm   Px   tt

Keeshond-colored wolf-sable:

a^wa^w Bx   Cx   Dx   Ex   Sx   gg   mm   Px   tt

True wolf-sable:

a^wa^w Bx $c^{ch}c^{ch}$ Dx   Ex   Sx   gg   mm   Px   tt

True beaver-colored:

A^sx   bb   Cx   dd   Ex   Sx   gg   mm   Px   tt

True blue:

| $A^s x$ | Bx | Cx | dd | Ex | Sx | gg | mm | Px | tt |

Black, after early puppyhood "blue" or gray:

| $A^s x$ | Bx | Cx | Dx | Ex | Sx | Gx | mm | Px | tt |

Red-sable or orange-sable:

| $a^y a^y$ | Bx | Cx | Dx | Ex | Sx | gg | mm | Px | tt |

(*Note:* A weakened gene a^y can also produce various dilutions of red, orange or even lightest cream, with or without sable markings.)

Black-and-tan:

| $a^t a^t$ | Bx | Cx | Dx | Ex | Sx | gg | mm | Px | tt |

White, of the German type:

| $A^s x$ | Bx | $c^w c^w$ | Dx | Ex | Sx | gg | mm | Px | tt |

Parti-colored (with black):

| $A^s x$ | Bx | Cx | Dx | Ex | $s^p s^p$ | gg | mm | Px | tt |

Parti-colored (with red-sable or orange-sable):

| $a^y a^y$ | Bx | Cx | Dx | Ex | $s^p s^p$ | gg | mm | Px | tt |

Parti-colored (with chocolate):

| $A^s x$ | bb | Cx | Dx | Ex | $s^p s^p$ | gg | mm | Px | tt |

Orange or red without sable markings or black pigment granules in the hair strand (black noses, eye rims and foot-pads):

| $A^s x$ | Bx | Cx | Dx | ee | Sx | gg | mm | Px | tt |

(*Note:* A weakened gene A^s may produce dilute orange shades or dilute red shades, even cream or almost white in a line, especially if both sire and dam possess this weakened gene A^s. Mating such a dog with another possessing a normal gene of the type a^y, a^t or a strong A^s can often greatly intensify, brighten and deepen the orange or red produced.)

Brown-nosed orange or red without sable markings:

| $A^s x$ | bb | Cx | Dx | ee | Sx | gg | mm | Px | tt |

Brown-nosed orange or red with chocolate-sable hair tips:

| $a^y a^y$ | bb | Cx | Dx | Ex | Sx | gg | mm | Px | tt |

Cream-colored:

A vast number of different possible combinations with various dilution patterns, too numerous to list here, are found in the Pomeranian of the color cream. Most cream-colored Pomeranians are probably dilute orange-sable or dilute orange, whereby the genes a^y and/or E are weakly functioning, or whereby the gene A^s is weakened, combined with the gene e. Also the genes c^{ch}, c^w, d, G or other modifying genes may cause a dilution to cream.

In Germany, it is only permissible to mate black to black, black to chocolate or chocolate to chocolate. Otherwise, only white to white, red (orange) to red (orange) or wolf-sable to wolf-sable matings are permissible, due to the strict rules of color breeding under supervision of a strict commission and registry.

If a black from a long line of black to black color breeding is mated with a chocolate, all the pups will probably be black, since the gene B of the black is dominant over the gene b of the chocolate.

If two blacks, both of which had a chocolate sire or dam, were mated:

$$A^sA^s \quad Bb \quad x \quad A^sA^s \quad Bb$$

then a ratio of three pups with the genes A^sA^s BB or A^sA^s Bb (black in coat color) to one pup with the genes A^sA^s bb (chocolate in coat color) can be expected.

If a black, one of whose parents was chocolate, is mated with a chocolate:

$$A^sA^s \quad Bb \quad x \quad A^sA^s \quad bb$$

then a ratio of one pup with the genes A^sA^s Bb (black in coat color) to one pup with the genes A^sA^s bb (chocolate in coat color) can be expected.

Germans have observed that only a dog with *intensely* pigmented, coal-black eyes and jet-black coat, derived from a chocolate to black breeding, can consistently produce, when mated with a chocolate, a generous share of the desired dark-chocolate pups. (Of course, as shown above, 50 percent of the pups from such a breeding will be blacks.) Matings of chocolate to chocolate are frowned upon, since both of these chocolate dogs could be carrying a dilution factor, which is not always easily detected in the chocolates. The pups could then turn out to be very *light* chocolate, which is not desired in Germany, since such coloring is usually accompanied by reddish "foxy" shadings. In a black, the dilution factors are usually readily noticeable through lighter brown eye coloring instead of black or a reddish-tinged black coat: the Germans refer to such a color as a "foxy black." Studs of the "foxy black" type may not be used for breeding. Thus, the best dark chocolates are almost always produced by mating two very intensely pigmented blacks, both of which had a chocolate parent; or by mating a chocolate with a very intense black, one of whose parents was a chocolate!

Although the wolf-sable color, as found in the Keeshond, has not been cultivated in the smaller Spitz varieties since World War II, a breeder will occasionally find a pup with that *original* Keeshond-colored type of wolf-sable in a litter from a black to black mating:

$$A^s a^w \quad BB \quad CC \quad x \quad A^s a^w \quad BB \quad CC$$

As is evident, both sire and dam are carrying the gene a^w. If a pup receives the gene a^w from *both* sire and dam:

$$a^w a^w \quad BB \quad CC$$

he will then be the Keeshond-type of wolf-sable in color. To produce a true wolf-sable, the gene for chinchilla-coloring ($c^{ch}c^{ch}$) would have to be present, additionally:

$$a^w a^w \quad BB \quad c^{ch}c^{ch}$$

(instead of the Keeshond-colored $a^w a^w \quad BB \quad CC$)

Mr. Ledbetter has certainly presented an in-depth discussion of Pomeranian coat color. Besides color, however, a Pomeranian breeder has to be concerned with the broader and nebulous aspects of breed quality. Breeding a healthy Pom of good type, coat and condition is not an easy task for anyone.

The standard says the Pomeranian should be "foxlike" in expression. John Heartz exhibits a fox for comparison.

Am., Can., and Bda. Ch. Millamore's Rock Medallion is definitely not a fox.

9

Breed Characteristics and Quality

COLOR COMBINATIONS ASIDE, breeding requires more than just selecting the nearest male or bitch, or even surmising that because a particular dog is doing a lot of winning at conformation shows it will, in turn, produce quality puppies. The breeding of good Pomeranians is a careful science that requires a thorough study of all aspects of both the bitch and stud. This study should encompass honest appraisals of each dog's positive and negative points, a review of the pedigrees, knowledge of the physical attributes of the animals in the bloodlines and an understanding of the personalities of the two dogs.

What is a quality Pom? A simple answer would be one that comes nearest to the breed standard. Nevertheless, a quality Pom can also be one that is a wonderful companion and loving pet while possessing only general attributes of designated breed type. The pet owner may believe that quality rests with an individual dog's ability to discern its master's emotional persuasion at any given moment.

Will the dog comfort its owner when the human has had a bad day? Will the animal keep him company when he is confined to bed with one illness or another? Is the dog there to share in moments of fun and gaiety? Will the pet make his master laugh and smile at its silly antics? For the average pet owner it is the personality of the individual dog that will make it nearest and dearest to the heart. This person often cares little how well the dog measures up to its breed standard just as long as it generally looks like a Pomeranian.

Breed Standard

For serious breeders and exhibitors of the conformation world, however, a Pom must do more than just look like a Pom. While personality and show presence are important, the way the dog measures up to its breed standard is what showing, or breed quality, is all about. The standard for the Pomeranian, presented by the American Pomeranian Club, Inc. and approved by the American Kennel Club on October 4, 1980, is:

Appearance—The Pomeranian in build and appearance is a cobby, balanced, short-coupled dog. He exhibits great intelligence in his expression, and is alert in character and deportment.

Head—Well-proportioned to the body, wedge-shaped but not domed in outline, with a foxlike expression. There is a pronounced stop with a rather fine but not snipy muzzle, with no lippiness. The pigmentation around the eyes, lips, and on the nose must be black, except self-colored in brown and blue. A round, domey skull is a major fault. Light pigment on nose or eye rims is a major fault.

Teeth—The teeth meet in a scissors bite, in which part of the inner surface of the upper teeth meets and engages part of the outer surface of the lower teeth. One tooth out of line does not mean an undershot or overshot mouth. An undershot mouth is a major fault.

Eyes—Bright, dark in color, and medium in size, almond-shaped and not set too wide apart nor too close together.

Ears—Small, carried erect and mounted high on the head, and placed not too far apart.

Neck and Shoulders—The neck is rather short, its base set well back on the shoulders. The Pom is not straight-in-shoulder, but has sufficient layback of shoulders to carry the neck proudly and high. Out at elbows or shoulders is a major fault.

Body—The back must be short and topline level. The body is cobby, being well ribbed and rounded. The brisket is fairly deep and not too wide.

Legs—The forelegs are straight and parallel, of medium length in proportion to a well-balanced frame. The hocks are perpendicular to the ground, parallel to each other from hock to heel, and turning neither in nor out. The Pomeranian stands well-up on toes. Down in pasterns is a major fault. Cowhocks or lack of soundness in hindlegs or stifles is a major fault.

Tail—The tail is characteristic of the breed. It turns over the back and is carried flat, set high. It is profusely covered with hair.

Coat—Double-coated; a short, soft, thick undercoat, with longer, coarse, glistening outer coat consisting of guard hairs which must be harsh to the touch in order to give the proper texture for the coat to form a frill of profuse, standing-off straight hair. The front legs are well feathered and the hindquarters are clad with long hair or feathering from the top of the rump to the hocks. A soft, flat, or open coat is a major fault.

Color—Acceptable colors to be judged on an equal basis; any solid color, any solid color with lighter or darker shadings of the same color, any solid color with sable or black shadings, parti-color, sable and black & tan. Black & tan is black with tan or rust, sharply defined, appearing above each eye and on muzzle, throat, and forechest, on all legs and feet and below the tail. Parti-color is white with any other color distributed in even patches on the body and a white blaze on head. A white chest, foot, or leg on a whole-colored dog (except white) is a major fault.

Movement—The Pomeranian moves with a smooth, free, but not loose action. He does not elbow out in front nor move excessively wide nor cowhocked behind. He is sound in action.

Size—The weight of a Pomeranian for exhibition is 3 to 7 pounds. The ideal size for show specimens is from 4 to 5 pounds.

Trimming and Dewclaws—Trimming for neatness is permissible around the feet and up the back of the legs to the first joint; trimming of unruly hairs on the edges of the ears and around the anus is also permitted. Dewclaws on the forelegs may be removed. Overtrimming (beyond the location and amount described in the breed standard) should be *heavily penalized.*

Classifications—The Open Classes at Specialty shows may be divided by color as follows: Open Red, Orange, Cream & Sable; Open Black, Brown & Blue; Open Any Other Allowed Color.

As with all standards, the words written therein are so stated to give the reader a view of the breed. Unfortunately, however, many times the view rendered by the necessarily briefly written standard needs to be explained, explored and examined in order to derive a clearer image of the breed. The Pomeranian standard is no different and an interpretative study that goes beyond the words in the standard is in order to help understand this breed.

Appearance—The Pomeranian is an alert, inquisitive, proud, square, small dog possessing a mischievous foxy expression and covered with a wealth of harshly textured guard hairs supported by a downy undercoat.

Head—There are many different types of Pomeranian heads, all of which someone or other will say has the called-for "fox-like" expression. Probably the best description would be to say that you do not want an exaggerated head, nor one that is tiny in relation to the size of the dog. Thus the words in the standard "well-proportioned to the body." The head, itself, should be wedge shaped with no evidence of an "apple dome." The stop is obvious to detect and the muzzle is fine without narrowing to snipiness. All pigmentation is black except for blue or brown Poms, who would have pigment the same color as their hair.

Teeth—A scissors bite, by AKC's description, is "the outer sides of the lower incisors touches the inner side of the upper incisors."

Eyes—Almond shaped, sparkling and dark adequately describes a proper Pom eye. The descriptions "medium in size" and "not set too wide nor too close" all signify that eye size and placement should be properly proportioned or harmonious in balance with the size of the head.

Ears—Ears should be set on top of the head, facing forward and proportionately small.

Neck and Shoulders—A short neck proudly carried high by a shoulder placement that is laid back behind the line of the neck.

Body—A short back and level topline encompassed by a rounded rib cage with a deepening, narrowing brisket.

Legs—Straight, parallel, proportionate in length to the size of the dog. Hocks are perpendicular to ground with sufficient stifle angulation to permit a smooth, free rear action. The Pom stands up on short, round compact feet.

Tail—The tail is set high, lies flat on the back over the spine and is profusely coated.

Coat—A Pomeranian is noted for its double-layered coat. The undercoat is soft, downy in touch, while the outer layer or guard hairs must be harsh. The undercoat and guard hairs must compliment each other. A thick undercoat will hold up and permit the guard hairs to stand-off from the Pom's body, forming a frill or halo around him.

Color—Acceptable colors are: any solid, any solid with lighter or darker shadings of the same color, any solid with sable or black shadings, parti-colors, sable and black & tan. These colors are to be judged as equals. If classes are divided according to color, care must be taken that the dogs are entered in the proper divisions.

Movement—A proper Pom movement is smooth, free and gay with neither an exaggerated hackney gait, nor one that drags or plods along. The dog will reach with his front legs and drive from the rear.

Size—A weight of 3 to 7 pounds is called for in the standard, with 4 to 5 pounds being given as the ideal weight for a show dog.

Written words, whether they appear in a breed standard or an interpretative study of the same, do not always suffice in conveying the mental picture of just what the Pomeranian is all about. Christine D. Heartz, Chriscendo Kennels, Nova Scotia, Canada—a

The ideal Pomeranian. *Heartz*

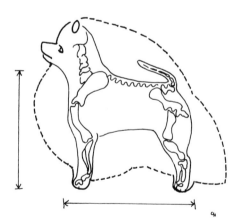

Skeletal view of the ideal Pomeranian.

Heartz

76

successful Pom breeder and talented artist—has drawn a series of Pomeranian sketches depicting the various positive and negative points of the Pom. Study these sketches and then actual dogs as a guide in understanding some of the basic breed elements and characteristics. Armed with a better and clearer awareness of Pomeranian traits, a breeder or exhibitor should be able to determine whether or not his dog possesses show and/or breeding quality.

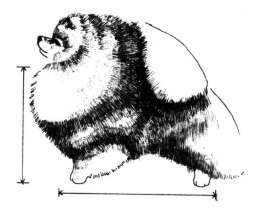

Long back, exaggerated stifles. *Heartz*

Straight shoulders with long back. *Heartz*

Low at the shoulders makes the animal look long in body.
Heartz

An overdone, heavy boned and headed Pom.
Heartz

The low tailset ruins the outline.
Heartz

A Pom with too much coat appears bigger and longer than he is. The dotted lines suggest possible lines for tidiness.   *Heartz*

A soft, thick coat on a correct body. Dotted lines suggest outline if the animal had the proper longer hair. *Heartz*

A soft, flat, open coat that lies on the body. *Heartz*

Ideal head, with good skull to muzzle, pretty almond eye, pleasing expression and nice ear size and placement. *Heartz*

Balanced skull with too small eyes and
lowset ears. *Heartz*

Balanced skull with not desired large,
rounded eyes and big ears. *Heartz*

Heavy, overdone head, often referred to
as "Chow" type. *Heartz*

Poor quality head, completely lacking in
breed type, long in muzzle, coarse,
downfaced. *Heartz*

83

Ideal head (profile), with good definition of stop, length of muzzle and adequate underjaw. (Note: lack of underjaw is a problem in some Poms. Too much underjaw leads to overshot bites.)

Heartz

Common head problems include ears too large, eyes round instead of almond shaped, longer muzzle, apple-domed skull and lack of underjaw. While this head may appear "foxy" to some, it should be noted that the standard refers to expression and not to conformation.

Heartz

Profile of a head lacking in good stop. Eye is too round. *Heartz*

Good side movement. *Heartz*

Lack of reach, paddling, wasted action. *Heartz*

Structurally correct frontal view.   *Heartz*

Out at the elbows.   *Heartz*

Fiddle front.   *Heartz*

Proper front movement.   *Heartz*

Out at the elbow movement.   *Heartz*

Weaving.   *Heartz*

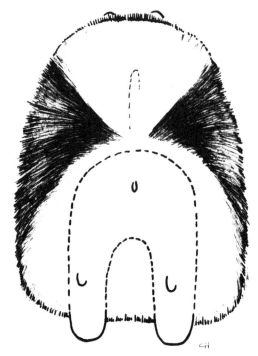

Structurally correct hindquarters.   *Heartz*

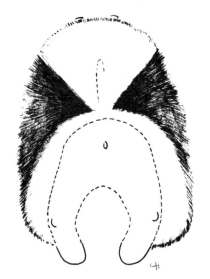

Wide in the rear.   *Heartz*

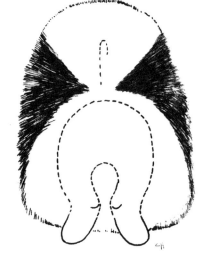

Cowhocked.   *Heartz*

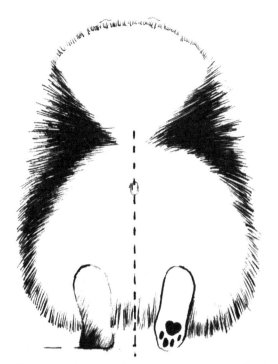

Proper rear movement.   *Heartz*

Wide rear movement.   *Heartz*   Weak rear movement.   *Heartz*

89

A family of Pomeranians: Ch. Jabil's Simply Scrumtious and Ch. Jabil's Italian Girl in Algiers lie beside their mother, Ch. Jabil's Simply Serena, right. Scrumtious and Serena are owned by Jessie and Barbara Young. Italian Girl is owned by Pam Welsh.

Wels.

10

Selecting a Mate

UNDERSTANDING A BREED STANDARD is but one vital aspect of selecting the proper stud. As previously mentioned, it is also necessary to know pedigrees, dominant and recessive traits within strains, physical positive and negative factors of the bitch as well as the prospective stud and a concept of exactly what you, the breeder, are looking for when you decide to mate two dogs.

Breeding for Quality

After carefully studying all the above, you will locate a male dog that you would like to have your bitch bred to. Alas, you may still have difficulties. Sometimes you may be hindered by tangible distances between where you reside with your bitch and where the stud lives. On other occasions, the stud fee may be more money than you can afford, or the owner of the male is unwilling to let the dog's services be used by outside bitches. If faced with one of these situations, you should return to square one and begin, once more, searching for another prospective stud.

What you should never do is just breed your bitch to the nearest Pom male, or to the top conformation winner just because you think that if that dog is good enough to do all that winning he must be able to pass his attributes on to his get. This is not necessarily true, nor would it always be certain that the winning attributes would be compatible with your bitch.

Good breeding tactics require careful strategy and honest evaluations of both dogs. If your bitch is long in body, you might want to select a male that comes from a line known for its fairly short back. If the bitch is coarse in head, a male with a good headpiece who comes from a line noted for correct heads would be the proper way to go. A shelly or slight-bodied bitch could be mated to a male who carries a strain known for its degree of substance and bone. There is no guarantee that the mating will produce puppies without the faults you are trying so hard to breed out, nor that the pups will not have received from the sire a whole new set of faults for you to contain. Nevertheless, with a conscientious analysis of the bitch, the prospective stud and the lines of both, a lot of patience and perseverance, and some good luck you should be able to improve upon what you already have. Studious, careful breeding is a necessity for a viable productive program.

Some of the best advice on breeding quality Pomeranians comes from successful breeders of today and years gone by. One such early English breeder, Miss Lilla Ives, wrote in her 1929 book, *Show Pomeranians,* the following thoughts, which still pertain today:

> The science of breeding may be reduced tersely in two golden rules: (1) The use of a stud dog which is a producer of typically well-coated stock; (2) the choice of a brood bitch not only bred from a few generations of reliable ancestry, but whose points, colour, and coat coincide with the standard arranged by the Pomeranian Club. The most desirable weight to breed from in bitches is between 5 and 7 lb. Little ones of 3 and 4 lb. should not be bred from at all. Neither should a shy bitch; no good results can be expected from such matings. These bitches are seldom good mothers, and their offspring usually inherit the dam's failings. An undershot bitch should also be avoided, the fault is very hereditary. Even though the bitch herself be a shade large,

if she comes from small ancestors her progeny may take after them. A brood bitch need not be a show bitch. . . .

The stud dog should be chosen well in advance and arrangements should be made with his owner sometime before the bitch is expected to be in season. When the first signs of this are detected notice should immediately be sent. . . . If she is to travel any distance . . . she should be forwarded to her destination at least two days before she is expected to be ready for service.

Breeding Methods

More recent thoughts on the subject appeared in the July and October 1981 issues of *The Pomeranian Review,* a quarterly publication published by the American Pomeranian Club, Inc. Written by Sophie H. Mayes, a noted Pom breeder (May Morning Kennels) and *Review* editor at that time, the articles entitled "Breeding Methods" present a concise and exceptionally informative study of linebreeding, inbreeding and outcrosses:

Before there was any knowledge of the science of genetics, persons wanting to breed dogs selected their breeding stock by method of mass selection, that is by trying to match or complement the breeding pair according to the appearance of the desired trait or traits in the individuals. Thus the cleverest sheep herders or the most aggressive fighters or the gamest terriers might be mated, without regard to pedigree (which often was unknown) or sometimes without regard to their apparent breed type. There were many failures. We now know that "phenotype" (appearance) is not a good indication of "genotype" (the genetic makeup which the animal can pass to its offspring). The old saying "like produces like" is only partially true. Dogs produce dogs (not kittens), Poodles produce Poodles, but alas for the hopes of many, champions do not invariably produce champions.

As the various breeds became more refined and better records were kept, another saying arose: "Don't breed to the Best in Show dog, breed to his sire." This was, in fact, not such a bad idea as it at least recognized that the sire possessed the genes that produced the Best in show specimen. And so breeders studying the ancestry or pedigrees of their breeding stock, still put much weight on the quality of the individuals to be bred.

Finally, as more and more became known of the whys and wherefores of breeding methods, it became obvious that the very *best*

93

way to select the perfect sire for a certain bitch was to look for a dog that had consistently produced highest quality offspring when bred with bitches whose pedigree was comparable to one's bitch's pedigree. This is called Progeny Selection.

The phone rings, you answer it and it is still another person inquiring for "just a pet, but it *must* be a female and yes, I might want to breed her." Patiently you explain that pet-quality Poms should *not* be used for breeding, etc., etc. Or perhaps the caller is a *Review* reader inquiring about some puppies you have advertised in the last issue. You answer the questions frankly and honestly, and then you do a little probing: if the caller is unknown to you, you would like to know how long he or she has been breeding Poms, what lines he owns, and what approximate plans he has for future breeding. In other words, if he buys the puppy will he know how to use it to his best advantage?

I am amazed—no, I am *appalled*—at the apparently endless number of would-be Pom breeders who undertake this important venture without any plan at all. (Needless to say, I am not talking about established breeders who would not have arrived at their established position without a definite breeding plan.)

AKC says a breeder is the owner or the lessee of the bitch when the puppies are whelped. But to me a Breeder (capital "B") is much more. A Breeder is a person who has studied and is constantly still studying every facet of the breed which he is trying to improve. This person has at least an elementary knowledge of genetics as it applies to dogs and to his breed in particular. He has a definite, preconceived plan of breeding and is objective enough to discard his breeding failures and start over if necessary. There is nothing worse than a kennel-blind breeder. Although he is able to produce good Poms, if he cannot tell the good ones from the bad ones, how in the world can he hope to improve?

Many of the would-be breeders tell me that they are going to "improve the breed and establish my own bloodline." Well! How are they going to go about it? In fact, do they even know that this "traditional" expression (bloodline) is about as erroneous as anything could be? Individual lines or strains are produced through genes, not the blood.

A complete understanding of the science of genetics is far beyond the scope of most dog breeders, but everyone undertaking to "improve the breed," as they say, or to produce the best possible specimens and not just churn out puppies to sell as pets should certainly make some attempt to understand and follow the simplest and most important rules of genetics. Read the articles on genetics in your dog publications—don't skip them because they are "hard to understand" . . . (read) books (on breeding and genetics).

Next—study pedigrees. The three-generation pedigrees printed in the *Review* are really not adequate for this purpose. It requires five generations for the degree of linebreeding or inbreeding, that is, the "trend" of the pedigree, to be understood. . . .

In studying pedigrees, it will soon become obvious that many of the champions are produced by linebreeding and inbreeding. In fact, and I cannot stress this too much, to establish your own strain or "line" of Pomeranians it is absolutely necessary to practice strict linebreeding, with perhaps a little inbreeding from time to time.

Let us first define our terms. To the geneticist there are only two methods of breeding: inbreeding and outcrossing. Inbreeding is the breeding together of related stock and outcrossing is the breeding together of animls for which no relationship can be found in at least five generations. Dog fanciers have modified these definitions (perhaps from an innate fear of the term "inbreeding"), and use the term "linebreeding" to indicate animals which are related to each other but excluding the very close relationships of father to daughter, mother to son and full sister to full brother. The closest relationships are designated "inbreeding" . . . .

Briefly, it should be crystal clear to everyone that if mating is made between litter brother and sister (inbreeding), because the sire of each is the same and the dam of each is the same, only half the number of different genes is encountered as when completely unrelated dog and bitch are bred together (outcrossing). What we call linebreeding lies somewhere in between these two extremes.

In order to establish a recognizable strain within the breed, it is necessary to concentrate the genes by breeding together animals related to each other and all tracing back to a common very excellent ancestor. The saying is: "It's what's up front that counts," and this means that practically no valuable genes are inherited from ancestors beyond the third generation. Consider: there are eight great-grand-parents and each animal possesses many thousands of genes. The next generation back consists of sixteen animals. Common sense tells us that the parents exert the most influence on the progeny, with a lesser percentage of genes inherited from the grandparents, etc. So line-breeding does not mean that two animals tracing back to the same distant ancestor, say in the fifth generation, are bred together, but that the relationship should be found within the first three generations.

A seven-generation or ten-generation pedigree is valuble for study, as it shows the "roots" or the foundation of the linebred

A study of May Morning (Sophie Mayes) Pomeranian heads: May Morning Gay Troubadour, Ch. May Morning Bravo Bravo and May Morning Concerto.

immediate ancestry. If the same famous champion appears in many different generations and is repeated again and again in the pedigree, this will show the direction or the trend of the breeding.

There is unquestionably an element of luck in dog breeding. Many times a breeding that looks absolutely "tops" on paper (reading the pedigree of the two just mated) will produce nothing but "junk." At other times, a less desirable breeding will "click" or in dog parlance "nick" and give you perfectly gorgeous puppies. That this is true is understandable when you realize that innumerable combinations of genes are possible when each animal possesses thousands upon thousands of these units of inheritance.

To establish a recognizable individual "strain" within a given breed, linebreeding is necessary. Hit or miss breeding between unrelated animals may give the breeder some excellent puppies (discussed more fully later under the heading of "Outcrossing"). But difficulties are encountered in the next and subsequent generations, when it becomes apparent that "scattering" of the genes has dispersed many of the good qualities first obtained, and a great variety of types is found, none of them anywhere near as good as either parent.

Linebreeding will act to concentrate the genes of the "prototype" excellent ancestor. This will "shorten the odds" for obtaining an equally excellent puppy. We have realized that breeding brother to sister will cut the odds in half, and this extreme form of inbreeding can be used by the daring breeder as a gamble to produce the very best. But the risks are great, as almost all "bad genes," that is faults, are recessive. In most cases, the dominant gene of a given pair will be the "normal," and the undesirable trait will be the recessive. This means that this particular fault will not show up unless and until it is found in *both* parents. If both parents have a recessive fault, a certain percentage of the puppies will receive a double dose of the recessive gene and the fault will surface. Certain colors are also known to be recessive, i.e. "covered up" by dominant colors until the recessive gene is found in *both* parents (chocolate, black and tan, etc.). Luxated patellas are recessive, but this fault is complicated by the fact that it is polygenic—that is, many different genes are involved, not just a single one. Thus, like hip dysplasia in larger breeds, luxated patellas cannot ever be completed eradicated by selective breeding. Cryptochidism is also recessive and apparently can be carried by females as well as males, although of course no female will ever have testicles so the genotype of female offspring can only be discovered by test breedings, not by appearance.

Inbreeding, then, is for the daring breeder who wishes to gamble *big.* A wise choice is linebreeding. Select for your breeding stock excellent quality individuals related to the same not-too-distant admired ancestor. I have found half-brother to half-sister, with the common parent being the better of the two if both are not equally good, an extremely useful breeding combination. Grandfather to granddaughter or uncle to niece can be equally good. First cousin to first cousin is O.K., but verging on the too distant relationship for best results.

Remember that in linebreeding and more so in inbreeding, the genes of the less-good ancestors will be concentrated just as surely as those of the best champions. This is *the reason* to start with excellent quality although not necessarily champion quality bitches for your breeding stock.

The English were and are marvelous dog breeders and we, especially, must give them credit for reducing size, improving and standardizing type and indeed for "creating" the modern Pomeranian. At first, their goal in breeding was to keep the colors "pure" and conformation was secondary to color-breeding. This changed about the time that we first began to import Poms in any great numbers, around the first of the century. The first imports were mostly blacks, whites, blues or chocolates of conformation that would not receive a second glance today. By the time imports ceased because of the First World War, conformation had become the primary consideration and sables and oranges were the most popular colors. It is an indisputable fact that if certain rare colors such as black, chocolate, white and blue are bred for color only to each separate color for several generations, conformation will revert to a much less desirable type than our present-day show Poms. We can only speculate why this is so. Perhaps there is a "linkage" of the genes, binding certain colors to certain types. In any case, color-breeding is a difficult and frustrating endeavor and is best left to the experienced breeders.

There are dangers as well as advantages to most worthwhile endeavors and the linebreeding of dogs is no exception. Although the risk is not quite as great as in close inbreeding, many times we are disappointed to find that our "perfect" breeding has brought together one or more recessive faults carried by the parents but unknown to the breeder until the two carriers were mated. Here is where the Breeders are separated from the puppy producers. Not only the end product of this breeding should be excluded from future breeding stock, but serious consideration (depending on the fault, the opposing good qualities of the pair, etc.) should be given to excluding the parents from the program also.

This brings us to the outcross method of breeding. There is an old saying, "Inbreed twice, then outcross." This is an *old wive's tale* that unfortunately persists along with the myths that feeding a dog sugar will give him worms and raw meat will give him "fits." A famous geneticist was asked by a novice breeder to write down the correct schedule for making an outcross. The man is supposed to have replied, "What utter nonsense! This is like asking me what day of the week to carry an umbrella!"

The fact is that in establishing a strain of Poms, an outcross should *never* be used, if it can be avoided. To my way of thinking, an outcross is either the breeding method of the ignorant novice or the cry for help for a more experienced breeder suddenly faced with a problem he thinks he can't solve within his own line.

As outcross breeding between two unrelated Poms is hybrid breeding, just as a breeding between a Peke and a Poodle is a hybrid breeding—the only difference is one of degree. The F_1 (first generation) offspring of a hybrid breeding will often show a spectacular quality which is often due to the mysterious but very real factor known as "hybrid vigor." We can find innumerable examples of this factor at work. The greatest boon to mankind in the past history of agricultural and other endeavors, before the advent of the gasoline and diesel engine, was the mule. As most of you know, the mule is the product of breeding a jack (male donkey) to a mare. Hybrid vigor insured that the mule was more resistant to disease and lameness and able to do more work on less feed and under more rigorous conditions than the horse. (What many of you may not know is that the result of breeding together a stallion and a jenny [female donkey] is an utterly worthless animal called the hinny.) Many are also familiar with the use of hybrid breedings in grains and in food animals to insure greater production or greater weight gain per pound of feed. The F_1 generation demonstrates the hybrid vigor mentioned above. Thus two different breeds of cattle are mated and the steers resulting are far superior to the pure-bred products. Hybrid corn often gives three times the bushels per acre over the individual parent stock. Many ornamental plants are improved in appearance or resistance to disease through hybrid breeding.

The mule is unable to reproduce himself as both male and female are sterile. Most but not all other hybrid animals and plants can reproduce, but for the most part the F_1 offspring are *not* used for breeding purposes as the results are almost invariably disappointing. In order to obtain more mules or more hybrid corn, etc., the original hybrid cross is repeated.

Jeremy's pedigree, showing an outcross on his dam's side.

CH. HI TIME SIMPLY JEREMY JABIL

Lou-Lan's Token of Friendship
CH. NANJO MASTERPIECE
Nanjo Jubilant
AM., CAN., BDA. CH. NANJO INTERLUDE
CH. THELCOLYNN'S TINY SUN DANCE
Thelcolynn's Tiny Treca
Thelcolynn's Tiny Karla
AM., CAN. CH. JABIL'S SIMPLY SMASHING
AM., CAN., BDA. CH. NANJO INTERLUDE
AM., CAN. CH. TOPAZE SIR BLITZEN
CH. TOPAZE DUCHESS OF JERIBETH
Jabil's Sun Goddess
CH. SCOTIA CAVALIER'S DREAM BOY
Jabil Petite Deliah, CD
CH. ROANOKE'S BAND BOX
CH. HI TIME SIMPLY JEREMY JABIL
CH. MAY MORNING BRAVO BRAVO
May Morning Social Lion
May Morning Alice
CH. THELDUN'S TIM DANDEE OF EDNEY
CH. BLAIR'S SOLITAIRE
CH. DUNN'S LITTLE TINA PRESHUS
May Morning Sweet May Ann
Edney's Sassy Samantha
Beisel's Wee Gold Flash
Beisel's Wee Flashie Red Man
Beisel's Lady Bombar
Edney's Taffy
Inky Waggn' Boy
Stafford's Little Mitt
Shawn's Star Bright

CH. GOLD TOY'S RED FLAME
Millamor's Gold Spice
CH. THELCOLYNN'S TINY SUN DANCE
Tina Marie VI
CH. THELCOLYNN'S SHOWSTOPPER
CH. DIVIE FLAME OF THELCOLYNN
Thelcolynn's Little Sir Dandy
Thelcolynn's Honey Bun
CH. NANJO MASTERPIECE
Thelcolynn's Tiny Tyeca
CH. JERIBETH'S DARLIN' DOODLE BUG
Jeribeth's Bitta Honey
CH. SUNGOLD GAY CAVALIER
Glad Day's Dream Girl
CH. RHELCOLYNN'S TINY SUN DANCE
Scotia Jimmy Jet's Cricket
CH. BLAIR'S SOLITAIRE
May Morning Suzie Q
CH. GREAT ELMS TIMSTOPPER AGAIN
Pomwin Busybody
CH. THELCOLYNN'S SHOWSTOPPER
Blair's Adorable Bit O'Gold
CH. MAY MORNING BRAVO BRAVO
May Morning Honey Chile
Beisel's Wee Gold Little Man
Beisel's Wee Lady Mischief
Caesar's Timothy
Kimp's Little Jill Flower
Pearl's Black Inkspot
Johnson's Pacer
Perrines Marvin
Shawn's Mischief

Simply Sinful is the offspring of a sire being bred back to its dam.

CH. JABIL'S SIMPLY SINFUL

        Lou-Lan's Token Friendship
     CH. NANJO MASTERPIECE
        Nanjo Jubilant
  AM. CAN. BDA. CH. NANJO INTERLUDE
        CH. THELCOLYNN'S TINY SUN DANCE
     Thelcolynn's Tiny Tyeca
        Thelcolynn's Tiny Karla
AM., CAN. CH. JABIL'S SIMPLY SMASHING
        AM., CAN., BDA. CH. NANJO INTERLUDE
     AM., CAN., BDA. CH. TOPAZE SIR BLITZEN
        CH. TOPAZE DUCHESS OF JERIBETH
    Jabil's Sun Goddess
        CH. SCOTIA CAVALIER'S DREAM BOY
    Jabil Petite Delilah, CD
        CH. ROANOKE'S BAND BOX
CH. JABIL'S SIMPLY SINFUL
        CH. NANJO MASTERPIECE
     AM., CAN., BDA. CH. NANJO INTERLUDE
        Thelcolynn's Tiny Tyeca
    AM., CAN. CH. TOPAZE SIR BLITZEN
        CH. JERIBETH'S DARLIN' DOODLE BUG
     CH. TOPAZE DUCHESS OF JERIBETH
        Jeribeth's Bitta Honey
Jabil's Sun Goddess
        CH. SUNGOLD'S GAY CAVILIER
     CH. SCOTIA CAVALIER'S DREAM BOY
        Glad Days Bream Girl
    Jabil Petite Delilah, CD
        CH. THELCOLYNN'S TINY SUN DANCE
     CH. ROANOKE'S BAND BOX
        Scotia Jimmy Jet's Cricket

Ch. Jabil's Simply Sinful is the sire. He is the product of close inbreeding—a son bred back to his dam.

Ch. Hi Time Simply Jeremy Jabil is half-brother to Sinful. He is the offspring of an outcross on his dam's side.

Ch. Daisy's Little Bit of Jabil is line related to both Sinful and Jeremy. All three males represent the same "type" of Pom and are owned by Jessie and Barbara Young.

Thomson

102

The reason the F_2 generation of hybrid breedings is disappointing is that the gene pool is scattered. We have lost the concentration of "good genes" that linebreeding or inbreeding brought us.

To bring this down to outcross breeding of Poms, the F_1 or first generation offspring of a complete outcross will often be a beautiful champion-quality animal. This is hybrid vigor at work. But since most Pom breeders are looking for long-term rather than just a short-term improvement, they will not expect the outcross champion to produce as well as the linebred champion. With too many outcross breedings the entire benefit formerly gained by linebreeding has been dissipated and lost.

There are prominent Pom breeders who have produced champion after champion by outcross or nearly outcross breedings. They have been "lucky" in achieving hybrid vigor and usually smart enough not to try to build a line on the results. Or where they have tried, they have failed and ceased breeding activities in disgust.

Outcross breeding cannot be used to correct a recessive fault and should not be thought of in that respect. Because the unrelated parents in a true outcross breeding very often do not carry the same recessive faults, the fault will be covered up or hidden in the offspring—but it is carried in many of the normal appearing animals and will reappear just as soon as an attempt is made to breed back into the linebred strain and once more concentrate the "good genes" in the line.

When a recessive fault appears, of course the breeding that produced it should not be repeated—unless the majority of the litter is free of the fault and perhaps one individual only need be "culled." Instead of resorting to a complete outcross, the breeder should attempt to compensate for the failure by breeding the normal appearing F_1 offspring to a mate in the same line, one that has never been known to produce this particular fault.

As a possible alternative, perhaps a partial outcross must be made, that is with only one-quarter of the pedigree of an outcross line, the other three-quarters linebred in the breeder's own line.

If a novice breeder has accumulated unrelated Poms all from good linebred strains, what course should be followed? If at all possible, *each* of these animals should be bred back into the strain from whence it came. This will give the breeder several different linebred strains from which to choose. While continuing to linebreed in each different strain, experimental (outcross) breedings can be made from time to time between two "families" of Poms, and thus several strains can be combined and subsequent generations bred

Multi-Best in Show winner Ch. Corn's Duke Dragonfly sired 34 champion offspring. Owned and shown by Darrell and Olga Baker.

One of Duke's many children was Ch. Duke's Lil Red Baron of O'Kala, 1971 Toy Group winner at Westminster. Owned by Ralph and Joyce Graves and shown by Sharon Dwyer.

back into alternate strains. It will quickly be noticed that certain strains seem to combine well and continue to show improvement in the F_2 generation and certain others show the disappointing degeneration commonly seen in outcross second generations. Keep the best and cull the rest.

Occasionally in color-breeding it is necessary to use an outcross breeding to find a mate of the desired color. In this case, the offspring should probably be bred back (inbred) to the parent or grandparent in the breeder's own strain known to carry the gene for that color if not actually of that color him/herself.

One last word: No method of breeding can be successful unless excellent quality breeding stock is used. Although a lucky fluke can certainly happen at long intervals, it would ordinarily take the whole lifetime of a breeder to upgrade mediocre pet stock to the point of consistently producing champions. So money spent wisely on foundation stock of best available quality will pay off in the long run.

Breeding Guidelines

The above advice is further expanded by these current observations of long-time, successful Pom breeders, Jessie and Barbara Young, Jabil Kennels, New Hampshire, who caution:

We believe absolutely in line and inbreeding. We also believe that such breeding should not be undertaken by a novice. Planning puppies involves risk, and, especially with inbreeding, the risk is that of intensifying faults. A person who plans litters plays God in doing so, and has to be absolutely honest about the faults and virtues of the breeding stock. Sometimes you go forward, and sometimes behind, but you must admit the faults or mistakes to go forward with regularity. You should also take stock of your kennel at times because while your dogs get better or sounder, cobbier, etc., you will find that a dog that was acceptable for breeding at one time may not fit into the program a few years hence.

Ch. Sungold's Wee Desire was one of Anna LaFortune's earliest Best in Show winning homebred bitches. *Ludwig*

Ch. Scotia's Pot O'Gold is one of Edna Girodot's homebred winners. He was handled by Frank Ashbey and William Kendrick is awarding the blue ribbon. *Brown*

11

Hints from Breeders

WHILE LINEBREEDING and inbreeding are methods that must be understood by anyone wanting to breed Pomeranians, so too must the concept of selection be understood. There are three common selection processes. One is known as phenotypic selection, or the selection of mates based on the appearance of particular traits in the individual dog. Those dogs that approach the considered ideal specimen are selected as breeding stock. Although one may expect some degree of gradual and consistent progress, one should also be aware that failures will result. This is because many beautiful dogs fail to pass on their fine features. Hence, a Best in Show dog may not always produce quality puppies.

Studying pedigrees and seeking common or compatible ancestors is another method used by breeders when selecting breeding stock. Again, one can expect a degree of success in procuring likeminded breed type. However, once again the risk is that the offspring will not enhance the line. Like does not always produce like.

The third, and perhaps best method, is one that combines physical characteristics, pedigree affinity and a thorough analysis of the existing progeny of the proposed breeding pair. The study of offspring gives a better idea of what characteristics the dogs are likely to pass on to their get.

Establishing a Breeding Program

Anna LaFortune, of the famed Sungold Kennels in California, offers these words of guidance for people wanting to breed quality Poms:

> Buy the best bitch that money can buy. Go to the shows to find out what line is winning and the type you like.
>
> No one is going to sell you their best producer, but maybe a pup out of her or her mother. Maybe you will only get two or three litters out of her, but it will be worth it. Keep nice typy females of 4½ pounds. Forget those long body 7½ pound girls because they will produce quantity and not quality. It's easy to sell two nice pups, but hard to sell five pet-quality pups.
>
> If you are going to be a small breeder, forget keeping or buying a male. The price of stud fees is easier than keeping a male that might not go with all your females.
>
> If you're going to start a large kennel, take a tablet and cut the pages in half. Put a three or four generation pedigree of the males on the top half and the girls on the bottom half. When a girl comes in season, turn the males' pedigrees over hers to see your best line-breeding. If she has a fault you must improve on, then find the male that has not produced these faults. This gives a good picture in your mind when you can see the pedigree. Bone structure is more important than a pretty face.
>
> Stay away from undershots and monorchids. Both these faults will come out someday in that super, super one you like the best. It leads to heartbreaks. Know what is behind your dogs and it will help a lot.

The genetic faults that Mrs. LaFortune refers to are heartaches in any breeding program. Monorchidism, the presence of only one testicle in the scrotum, and cryptorchidism, the presence of no testicles in the scrotum, are inherited traits that should be avoided. Once in a line, these traits are extremely hard to breed out. The American Kennel Club demands that all males exhibited at dog

Ch. McKamey's Sundown Commander was an outstanding sire owned by Anna LaFortune and bred by Mrs. Norris McKamey.   *Ludwig*

One of his get was Ch. Sungold Gay Cavilier, shown at ten months of age. He was bred by Anna LaFortune and sold to Edna Girodot of Scotia Kennels. Cavilier went on to become the top-producing sire of all times—a record that still holds.   *Ludwig*

shows must have two testicles of normal size located in the scrotum. It should be noted that floating testicles, or those that can be pulled up because of fear, cold or anything else are not considered "normal." Many breeders believe that male dogs who are abnormal should never be shown or bred. Instead, steps should be taken to find a good, secure pet home for the animal.

Another of Mrs. LaFortune's remarks dealt with the subject of size. She stressed the point that large bitches should not be used for breeding just because they are big and will produce a quantitative number of puppies. Breed quality is what should be sought and just as a bitch can be too big and coarse in bone, she also can be too small to produce puppies without veterinary assistance. Diminutiveness is not considered a quality or even desirable trait. Producing too many tiny Poms who cannot safely reproduce will eventually lead to the demise of the breed.

Any breeder or breeder-to-be should always keep in mind two paramount thoughts that should be considered above all else: (1) the health of the bitch and (2) the breed quality of her expected progeny.

Edna Girodot, Scotia Kennels, attributes her success at having bred over 150 champions to a worthwhile breeding program that she improved upon once her line had been stabilized:

> I tried to breed for quality—keeping records. I found out that after getting proper stock on hand a half sister and brother, aunt and uncle, mother and grandson, and granddad and granddaughter produced the best puppies. Sometimes I bred out and then brought these pups back in. In breeding, it was my policy to breed a dog or bitch weak in something to a mate that would compliment that fault. Trial and error is necessary at all times. Persistency is an asset in any breeding program. Never give up!

Becoming a breeder of quality Pomeranians is not an easy task for anyone to undertake. Even those who have long been successful have occasionally muttered, "I'm going to quit. It's too hard, too heartbreaking. I'll buy what I need." But breeders are the backbone of any breed and if everyone gave up, where would they turn when they want a new puppy? And what about the personal satisfaction of having bred that "beautiful dog," or of being able to conquer nature and raise a sickly puppy to become someone's lovely pet? Being a breeder is difficult, no one will deny that, but the rewards of the quest many times surpass the hardships and heartaches involved. Sally Baugniet, of the Pomirish Kennels in Wisconsin, describes her feelings when she says:

> The uncracking of the stiffening joints in trying to get up from the floor after breeding these little beauties; the all-night vigil to watch the bitch whose whelp is imminent; the occasional, and sometimes not so occasional, trip, usually in the middle of the night, to the veterinarian for a C-section; the extra care of the bitch and puppies needed after the operation; and sometimes the many round-the-clock days and nights of tube or bottle feeding for puppies who wouldn't make it without you, make the Pomeranian breeder a very special breed of the human race.
>
> Many people looking to purchase a show-quality Pom, or even requesting a group competition winner, do not realize the hours dedicated to the little 4 or 5 pound Pom by the breeder. Some expect to get this quality for "peanuts." No wonder you hear a breeder say, "I've had enough. I'm not breeding anymore. If I want one, I'll buy it." How many of us have either said this or at least thought about it?
>
> I have, and yet there is nothing more satisfying than a breeder seeing a dog he/she had bred, win in the ring, finish its championship, even placing in the Group, and heaven forbid, go Best in Show. It is a thrill to be breeder-owner of such a Pom, but there is nothing more ultimate, in my opinion, than being the breeder-owner-handler of that Pom. *Somebody* has to be breeder! Why not me?

Beautiful homebred puppies, such as Ch. Pomirish Scooters Victory (at six months of age), make Sally Baugniet of Pomirish Kennels glad she's a breeder. *Meyer*

112

12

Becoming a Breeder

EXPERIENCED BREEDERS know that it is not easy to select a male, breed a bitch, whelp a litter and successfully raise a bunch of healthy, quality puppies. Anyone desiring to venture on such a journey should educate themselves by reading the general topic literature that can be found in book stores, at dog show concessions and in dog-related magazines (see the Appendix for a list of suggested readings). Read breed magazines and columns, talk with knowledgeable breeders and make copious notes on anything and everything. Many successful oldtimers have mastered the craft by listening to what others have done, by practicing and, in some cases, by learning the hard way what to do and not to do in a given situation.

Once pedigrees have been studied, any known offspring scrutinized and both the bitch and prospective sire carefully analyzed for breed type, possible inherited traits and overall condition, the breeder-to-be is on his or her way.

Breeding Guidelines

There are some basic guidelines that knowledgeable breeders

Before a bitch is used for breeding she should be in good health.

always keep in the back of their minds for ready reference:

1. After the bitch in season has first begun to noticeably bleed, seven to ten days may pass before she will be willing to accept a stud dog.
2. More than one breeding should take place. If time permits, two or three breedings are preferred, with the second and third matings taking place at 48-hour intervals.
3. Let the bitch and stud get together to acknowledge each other before attempting to mate them.
4. Keep careful records of all breeding dates.
5. 63 days is considered the normal gestation period, but watch the bitch for whelping signs as early as day 57 and as late as day 67.
6. A bitch will carefully prepare a "nest" or shred papers before going into labor.
7. The dog's temperature will drop from the normal 101° to 102° F, to below 100° F. The drop usually occurs within 24 hours of labor.
8. If she is having problems—straining hard and getting nowhere, straining and then totally quitting, doing absolutely nothing—call your veterinarian and describe what is or is not happening.
9. The veterinarian may want to see the bitch and give her an oxytocin shot to bring on natural whelping, or may decide that a Caesarean would be safest for both the bitch and her puppies. Listen carefully to what he or she says and use your judgment.

Veterinary Guide for C-Section Delivery

If the bitch has to have a Caesarean and the veterinarian is not familiar with the Pomeranian, Dr. Glenn R. Popp, of Manitowoc, Wisconsin, the veterinarian for Dick and Sally Baugniet's Pomirish Kennels, offers this technique:

4-5 lb. Pom. 1/4 cc. Innovar + 1/2 cc. (.25 mg.) Atropine intra-

"Calvin" is a blooming ten-week-old Chriscendo puppy.

At six months of age, Chriscendo Captivation displays beautiful Pomeranian type that would satisfy all breeders.

venously. Then approximately 3 cc. Lidocaine is used to freeze abdominal incision site.

This technique on Caesareans has proven safe and effective for me over the years. I attach 1 cc. of suital to the I.V. leg in case I need more anesthetic, but rarely have to use any as it will depress the pups more.

At the conclusion of surgery or in respiratory arrest problems (also rare with this technique) the Innovar can be reversed with 1/4-1/2 cc. Naloxone I.V. The Naloxone at the conclusion of surgery speeds up the wakening process and mothering ability of the bitch, although many of the bitches are alert enough at the conclusion of surgery that Naloxone isn't necessary.

A bitch, and her puppies, brought home after a C-section should be carefully watched. They need to be kept warm, quiet, comfortable and loved.

A new litter of Pom pups with their contented mother.   *Welsh*

13

Whelping the Pomeranian

ONE OF THE BEST articles ever written about whelping the Pomeranian appeared in *Pomeranian Review,* the magazine of the American Pomeranian Club, Inc. It was first printed in the April and June 1977 issues and then reprinted in the Anniversary Issue 1958–1978. Written by Elma Maines, the article offers an excellent reference on whelping Poms:

> There are breeders of Pomeranians more experienced and more qualified to write about the whelping of puppies than I am. However, I find very little information in print regarding the whelping of Pomeranians. First, let me say, I have had no veterinary training or schooling, I am just trying to help someone else from experiences I have had myself. I write with the hope perhaps it would help someone who has an emergency facing him. It seems that when trouble comes it is usually after midnight or on a weekend, especially if my veterinarian is out of town.
>
> I learn something from each whelping and I find myself worrying and watching each mother whether she is whelping for the first time or is a veteran. For we all know, a bitch that has whelped several times without any trouble at all, can suddenly come up with a big problem. For example, a breech presentation with the puppy upside down

demands action in a hurry and you may not be able to contact your veterinarian to help in time.

Needless to say, you should be prepared, read, read, read, to learn all you can about whelping. If you can't find a suitable Pomeranian book in your library read any book on Toy breed whelping. Then assemble the necessary equipment at least a week ahead of time. You will need a whelping box—a cardboard box from the grocery store will do providing it is about 16 × 24 or so. Encourage your expectant Mama to sleep in this box, let her know it is hers. A long slender box enables a Mama to feed her babies and then move to the cool end of the box away from the heat, while the babies sleep on a warmer bed. They quickly learn to crawl to her to eat and back to the warm spot to sleep. Have clean baby blankets, an old sheet made into a pad, etc., and put a thick layer of newspaper on the floor of the box under the bedding to insulate from the cold. Keep in mind this first bedding will be thrown away, or washed after whelping as it will be wet and soggy. Therefore, a new pad of material tiny feet can get traction on will be necessary after all the puppies are delivered. Be careful not to use something a tiny puppy can get into the folds of and get smothered or crushed by the Mama. You will need sterile scissors, cool sterile water, alcohol for sterilizing, thread of tying naval cords, several sterile wash cloths, medical soap (from druggist), a couple of hemostats or forceps for clamping cord ends, a good electric heating pad or hot water bottles, an eye dropper or tiny pet nursing bottle, or even equipment for tube feeding just in case you have to feed the puppies. I suggest you have a notebook to keep track of each puppy— time of birth, sex, color, weight, etc. Try to note the very first contractions, the first sighting of the water bag, the first appearance of the puppy, etc. In case of trouble your veterinarian will want to know all of these things, and you will want them for your permanent record on that bitch.

When you know time is getting close, clip the hair from the mother's tummy and breasts so they are easily accessible to tiny babies. Also clip the hair around the vulva and keep the area clean with soap and water and at least towel dried. If your bitch is very heavy, she may have a slight mucous show from the vulva just before the puppies are born. If you start checking a week before due date, you will find your mama-to-be's normal temperature is about 101.5°. When time gets near check daily and about 12-24 hours before labor begins you will probably find a temperature drop to about 98° or even 97°. It is nearly impossible to tell from a bitch's behavior just when she is actually going to go into labor. You can look at her and she will seem normal and then if you go to the store for a little quick shopping you can come home and find a couple of puppies already there, or a bitch in trouble. So the best test is temperature, and when it is down try to keep special surveillance.

Some females are very calm and some very agitated, tearing wildly at their bedding, perhaps changing from the box to the closet if you don't keep that door shut, and watch they don't get into an arm chair or even on your bed. When a toy dog is whelping you must realize they are much slower than larger dogs. Give them time and the Pom will usually deliver with very little, if any, help. I am in favor of as little interference as possible, but sometimes you just have to do something to help out.

It is helpful to know when the first real contractions begin. Real contractions are unmistakable. You will see the dam tense, hunch up, then strain and then relax. This is repeated over and over as the puppy is pushed along to the cervix opening. It may take about an hour after the first contractions for the water bag to appear. After that she may take another hour of labor to produce the first puppy, but by now she has usually settled down to the task at hand. Continuous heavy contractions of 2-3 hours or so without any result call for a veterinarian's help. Needless to say a Pomeranian prefers her home for whelping, not a veterinarian's office, but sometimes a pituitary shot will pop a puppy right out, or the veterinarian's experienced hands can help a hung-up puppy out quickly. Also, your veterinarian will know when a Caesarean section is necessary. Never attempt to use any instrument to deliver a bitch.

In normal delivery a puppy follows the water sac in time. It emerges nose first with front feet under the chin, its back in line with the mother's back, belly down. If the head emerges, at long last, and there is just the head, no front feet, and the bitch keeps trying and the contractions are strong but no more progress is seen, you must help. Wash your hands in the sterile water and then with soapy hands and fingers (soap is antiseptic and a lubricant) you will have to insert a finger into the vulva, slowly and gently, down the puppy's chest and to one side, as the puppy's front feet are down increasing the girth of the chest, feel for a front leg, catch it under the puppy's armpit and draw it out; now reach in again and bring out the second front leg. The puppy will most likely pop right out now. You may have to help a little by very gently, persistently putting a wee bit of pull as the mother strains to get the shoulders and then the hips out. Keep your eye on the clock to see how much time is going by, don't be in too much of a hurry. Puppies can be lost from hurrying too much, too.

If this is the bitch's first litter, or if she is very tired or suffering from shock, she may not clean her puppy when it arrives. If she does not, you will have to do the job. Usually the sac breaks very easily, sometimes it is quite tough. If the afterbirth (placenta) comes out easily pull gently and get the puppy out of the sac, wipe away the fluid from the puppy's mouth and nostrils. Many use a soft ear syringe for this; if you are a beginner be careful. If it gasps and begins breathing and crying naturally, its lungs have filled with air and all is well. However, if the placenta has not come loose, stubbornly resisting a gentle pull, you will have to use your clamping hemostats and put one 3/4 inch from the pup's belly and the other as close to the mother's body as you can. Cut the cord between clamps with a chewing, not clean sharp cut; don't let that cord disappear back up into the mother if you can help it, keep that hemostat clamped on the cords ends. If it should break again and if there is any sign of it, keep insistently tugging at the threads of it gently and it will probably come free. If it does not come out it can cause a lot of trouble, by impeding the progress of the next oncoming puppy. Keep track of it if you can, if you think it has not come out you will need a veterinarian to give the bitch a shot to expel the placenta. Keep track—there is a placenta for each puppy.

If the puppy has stayed limp and flabby, and appears dead, attention to the puppy is of first importance. **Always** think of it as alive—towel it, rub it vigorously, hang it head downward. If it still does not gasp for air you should cradle it head down in the palm of your hand, with its back against your hand, with your other hand over the puppy and raise it shoulder high and gently swing it downward in a sweeping arc a few times, or until you hear it cry. This will expel any fluids and air will fill its lungs. When the lungs inflate the muscles of the puppy will draw up and the puppy will seem to shrink in length and it will now feel firm and plump. If you have not already done so, cut the cord now. If there seems to be no further breathing problem give it to its mother.

The mother will defecate the puppies by licking. The kidney action readily starts with stimulation. You will notice the mother stroking the anal area and the puppy will strain and a string of brown beadlike membrane will emerge. If for some reason you must care for the puppies yourself you will have to see to this task. Stroke the puppy in both areas with a small piece of cotton dipped in warm water. Be sure the bowels and kidneys work with each feeding. If the anal area is allowed to remain unexpressed a full day, the feces will dry into a hard mass and become very hard to remove. A clogged bowel will cause death in a couple of days.

If the puppies are a bit premature or for some reason the milk flow is slow in coming, a few drops of honey water or karo water will tide the puppies over for a short time. If the milk flow is delayed 6-8 hours a veterinarian can give the dam a shot to start the milk flow. Keep in mind the first 36 hours of its life the puppy absorbs antibodies from the colostrum which gives it protection from diseases. If the puppies do not receive this colostrum from the dam you should start immunization at a very early age. My veterinarian says the colostrum is absorbed only the first 36 hours of the puppies' life and that a foster mother lactating several days previous to these puppies' birth does not have the colostrum left for the new foster puppies.

Watch the flow from the dog's vulva for the next several days. A normal flow of bloody mucus is expected, but a dirty brown or greenish discharge calls for your veterinarian's advice. It is wise to check the dam's temperature daily for a few days after the puppies arrive. Keep an eye, too, on the puppies. They should gain daily and be plump and firm. Weigh them if you have scales and record their progress. If a puppy doesn't gain quickly, or if the skin will pinch up in your fingers, it may be dehydrating. It may be the heating pad is too warm; it should be just barely warm to touch, not hot. If you think something is wrong with puppy or dam see your veterinarian. . . .

[This material] should be regarded as an aid in enabling one to cooperate intelligently with a veterinarian if his assistance is needed. Or, should you find that you need to help the dam before a veterinarian's help can be received. Never hesitate in calling a Vet, or begrudge his fee; your little prospective puppies are valuable and your bitch is priceless, sentimentally if not financially. Just one puppy saved or the life of your beloved bitch will pay the fee many times over.

I feel a breeder should be able to take over and assist a whelping dam to prevent her suffering or from losing a whelp, as many times a veterinarian cannot be reached in time to save a puppy. My first experience in pulling a puppy was while in a veterinarian's office. The veterinarian was doing surgery and could not stop; my dam's pelvis was narrow and the puppy was large. The puppy's head had been out for approximately half an hour and the cask was broken, and the dam was making no further progress, with the contractions still strong. The puppy's front feet were not showing and I knew I could not just take hold of the head and pull as I might break the puppy's neck. Finally, after waiting too long to suit me, I got up my nerve and set a towel I had brought along on a table and put the dam on this and placing my fingers on either side of the puppy's head and then up into the vulva I surrounded first one front leg and pulled it out and then the other. Then sliding the fingers back behind the shoulders I pulled the puppy out with the dam's contractions helping. A second puppy arrived about 15-20 minutes later, in the treatment room this time, as the office girl conceded this was an emergency.

Pomeranians have many varied behavioral mannerisms so there is no exact science to whelping. A normal gestation is 63 days; however, whelping may occur in 57 days or run 2-3 days overtime. Early miscarriage is rare, but can happen from some medical problem or injury. In this case puppies may be too weak or immature to survive. If a bitch is more than 3 days overtime something may be wrong so consult your veterinarian.

Just as the dam is about to whelp she will refuse food—she will often vomit if she has recently eaten. She will start panting and usually not settle down unless you sit down with her. The vulva will soften and a mucous discharge may appear. She will get in her box (if previously introduced to it and has been made to feel it is hers). She will start hunching, then straining and then relaxing over and over again. She may turn her head about anxiously looking at her rear parts. She will press hard against the sides of her box with her hind feet. When these first strains start mark the time down; you may forget in the excitement if you don't. You can write your observations on the side of the box she is in at the time and copy them down in your permanent records later, as you may lose track of a notebook if the delivery is long or gets complicated.

Now the labor has started and may last from as little as 20 minutes to several hours. I usually find approximately 1 to 1½ hours from first labor contractions to the water bag. It may take another hour until the first puppy, Pomeranians dilate very slowly, and still another hour to the next puppy, etc., but this is by no means the rule. It may take more or less time. A dam may take naps between contractions and there is no need to worry at this. The time to worry is when the contractions are strong and close together for 2-3 hours and no progress is being made. You may be in for an abnormal whelping if this occurs and you may want to call your veterinarian. (Also, if actual labor stops.)

After long hard laboring you may find that the puppy is presenting backwards (breech). Usually puppies come into this world head first, belly down, with the back in line with the dam's. Puppies vary greatly in size at birth and a large puppy and a small dam with a narrow pelvis is a poor combination. When a breech birth is experienced, given a bit of time your dam may produce the puppy without any help. However, if the dam has been working very hard and finally you can see the puppy's hind feet, and after many hard contractions that is all you can see, or if the hind feet seem to come out a bit and then recede you may want to help the dam yourself. Hopefully you have assembled emergency equipment a week ahead of time and have it sterile and waiting. . . .

If you find the contractions are seemingly useless and you can see two hind feet (or perhaps can only feel them in an enclosed sac), grasp them with a sterile wash cloth and hold them so they will not slide back into the dam as the contractions lessen. If the puppy still does not come, put her (the dam) up on a table with a clean rug or blanket to help you work easier. Your bitch will be very nervous and may resist; control can be gained by holding her tail and then getting her between your arm and your body. For this procedure you may need a helper to hold the female in a standing position. We wait for the intermittent straining, push apart the lips of the vulva with the left hand from above the dog, with the index finger and thumb on one side and the other three fingers on the other side. Using a newly sterilized finger with an encircling motion work up into the vulva and try to move up and around the thighs and rump of the puppy using some lubrication (soap suds, oil, etc.). When you have brought down the puppy's tail and the hips and the bulk are out, give the dam a few moments and she may expel the puppy now without further help. If not, you must work a couple of fingers around the puppy's rump to the flanks and pull gently as the dam strains. The pull should be outward and slightly downward. The puppy now must come out.

You will not injure the dam if you work gently with sufficient lubricant and the puppy will most likely survive if you get it out quickly enough. A minimum delay is necessary in a breech delivery for if the sac covering the puppy is torn the puppy may drown, or if compressed in the birth canal too long it will die. Regardless, if you have no veterinarian on hand it is better to get a breech puppy out dead or alive, and you may save other whelps to come, or even the bitch. Some puppies are exceptionally strong and will survive an unbelievable length of time and some are lost in a very short delay in delivery.

A complication that is not often encountered is an "upside down" presentation. This can happen with head or breech delivery and one should get to a veterinarian if possible. This article is written, however, for someone not able to reach a veterinarian and with the encouraging thought that we have seen them completed with live puppies to reward our efforts. This complication is of the feet, belly and head pointing upwards against the roof of the dam's pelvis. I had one female deliver two in this manner without any help whatsoever. However, I have had to deliver two breech and one head presentation in this upside down manner and all survived. The whelping of the bitch is much the same as with other deliveries except that you must exert any tension or "pulling" outward and upward at about a 45° angle instead of outward and downward. If a breech upside down presentation occurs the feet will probably be tucked under, or backwards on the belly and only a rump or tail is seen. You must draw the feet to their correct position one after the other—give the dam a moment, she may expel it herself. If not grasp the feet and with an outward and upward tension work the puppy out. The puppy may "hang up" at the rib cage and need a little extra work getting it coming again. At this point you may be able to turn the puppy to its proper downward position, but do not spend too much time at trying this as by now it is nearly there and with a bit of more upward urging it should come.

If you have an "upside down" head presentation the front feet will most likely be tucked down on the chest instead of out under the chin. This gives it much more girth and you will have to reach in and work first one front leg out and then the other. This may be enough to let the puppy slide on out. If you still must pull remember to pull upward and outward. After the puppy's chest is out it usually comes quite easily. If it turns to proper position at this point you can pull downward. If it doesn't turn but still has its feet pointing towards the ceiling keep urging it out with upward and outward motion. These are severe manipulations and one's best friend at this time is a veterinarian, but if necessary you can do it if you just get hold of your nerve and do it. Needless to say, you should have your little mother examined after such an experience, and she will most likely need antibiotics. Keep a close watch on her, take her temperature a couple of times a day. Feed her good nutritious food, but do not over do it with a lot of rich food she is not accustomed to, as you can add a bad case of indigestion or diarrhea to her already traumatic experience.

14

Whelping Tips

PREPARING FOR WHELPING is always an anxious time for the new breeder. Not only must the bitch be attended to, but the puppies that are born need careful and close supervision. The best way to learn about taking care of new mothers and puppies is to speak with experienced Pom breeders who are willing to describe their own trials and tribulations, as well as offer support and guidance. One such successful, experienced breeder willing to share her thoughts and suggestions is Anna LaFortune of Sungold Kennels:

> My mother-to-be is due next week. She is brought into the bedroom after having been cleaned. She is bathed and her stomach is washed with a paste of baking soda water and shaved. Her ears are checked and cleaned for any ear mites. Her teeth are cleaned and the mouth swabbed with peroxide.
>
> I put her in a large cardboard box with a smaller box placed inside it. She is taken out to exercise in a pen three times a day. She walks where no other dog has walked. A pinch of salt is added to her meals. This makes her drink more water so that she will have plenty of milk.

The week has passed. My mother is digging a nest in the papers that line her box. Her temperature is 98°. A small wash cloth and scissors which have been disinfected with rubbing alcohol have been placed nearby.

A dark brown bag or sack begins to make its appearance. Two feet are coming in the bag. I hope the bag doesn't break because the pup could drown. If the bag breaks, I'll have to quickly pull the puppy out and take a chance on rupturing its navel. So, I press her tummy with each pain to ease the puppy along. The pup is born in the sack and my mother quickly takes care of it. I let her eat the afterbirth, being careful that she doesn't choke on it. I dry the puppy and put him in a tiny box in a warm place.

Mother is in labor with the next pup. Head first this time and when he finally comes out, she's too worried about the first one to bother with him. I break the sack and pull it off the head and down over the pup's body. I cut the cord, but don't tie it. I won't let my mother eat more than one afterbirth and I don't tie the pup's navel because I believe it fills up with fluid if you do, causing infection to set in. Also, if she got in trouble I have to know for sure the pups are lined up and she's opened. I feel that a pit shot if things are not right can cause broken necks on pups and bad uteruses for mothers.

This boy is put in with his brother. Mother is washed and blown dry. The little box is taken out and a kitty litter box is put in a pillow case so pups cannot get under it.

Both pups are given one drop of liquid antibiotic for the first three days. At birth, 3 oz.; at one week, 6 oz. Pups doing normal. At five weeks, the pups are given a mixture of Pablum Rice Cereal, Karo syrup and Pedicalyte, which is mixed in a fine gravy for them to easily lap without choking.

It is wonderful to swim in and see how dirty they can get. I clean them with baking soda and begin to brush them. I also do this if I see a flea.

Now my pups learn to eat. Baby beef or lamb is added to the rice mixture. After a while, they start eating mother's food.

One isn't doing well and doesn't want to eat. I give him some Nutri-Cal, approximately an inch worth from the tube. The next day, the pup is lying on his side. 1 cc. of Pedicalyte and Nutri-Cal is put in his rectum. He is not coming around. He cannot swallow. I put my finger in the Karo bottle and rub the Karo syrup on his gums about five times. The pup starts to come around. Nutri-Cal is given in the mouth. Twenty minutes later he is in fine shape once more.

Mother just sleeps with her pups now. The teeth are well in, so

128

mother doesn't want them and they don't need her. She is given a booster shot, combed out good and returned to her normal life.

The pups at three months are still cute, both short and nice. At four months, they begin to look raggy. I comb and remove all loose coat. The nails are cut from the time they were one week old and then every two weeks thereafter for a nice foot.

Pup No. 1 has both testicles, but pup No. 2 only has one. I start 1/2 tablet Winstrol V (2 mg.) twice a day for six weeks and every time I can, I pull on the testicle that is not yet down.

The teeth are beginning to change. I pull all six of the top teeth, all teeth between the K-9s. I pull the baby K-9s only when the permanent ones are in fully. The roots on baby teeth are unbelievable, so K-9s must be pulled.

Oh, No! Puppy No. 1 has a pink looking foot and he's been biting on it. I take a baby food jar, put in 30 parts water to 1 part bleach and put his foot in it every day for four days. The problem clears right up. This is the first sign of foot fungus, even in grown ones.

At four months old, I had two nice short males, but at six months old pup No. 2, now with both testicles down, has gone long in body. I would not buy or sell a male for show purposes unless he was at least six months old. The months between four and six are when puppies tend to look their worst and any and everything happens to them.

A lot of people may not agree on feeding salt, but I've never had a mother that didn't have plenty of milk and never had one have a heat stroke.

If you have a pup born that doesn't want to start breathing, instead of breathing into its mouth place hot tap water (but not scalding) and ice water into two separate containers. Holding the pup by the head, dip him into first one and then the other counting up to three each time. The pup will quickly yell and start to breathe.

I use two drops of Donnatal Elix for puppy bloat.

A young pup shares his basket with an abyssinian cat.

Puppies snuggle up to anything, even a teddy bear. *Welsh*

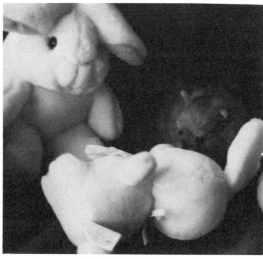

A healthy puppy likes to explore.

15

Puppy Health Problems

BREEDERS AND OWNERS of young puppies should keep a close watch for any signs of physical distress or disorder in their dogs. Being alert to early symptoms and getting prompt veterinary assistance can often keep illnesses from becoming life threatening.

Fading Puppy Syndrome

The Fading Puppy Syndrome is a term used to describe the sudden fading away of puppies during the first six weeks after birth for no obvious, apparent reason. Puppies plagued with Fading Puppy Syndrome usually are limp, cold and pot bellied, and they squirm a lot and cry. They also are generally rejected by their mothers and will refuse to nurse. Any breeder faced with a puppy who suddenly fades has a challenge ahead to save the pup.

The sick puppy should be taken away from its mother and steps must be taken to try to return the cold pup to normal heat. One of the best ways to do this is to hold the puppy close and heat it through human body heat. Not only will the puppy receive warmth, but also some kind of an inherent strength from the comfort and closeness of another living entity.

The puppy's food can be supplemented by a product manufactured as a supplemental mother's milk, such as Esbilac. An eye dropper, child's play baby bottle or small animal nipple bottle can be used to feed the pup. In all cases, care must be taken to give the pup only a small amount of liquid at a time so that it does not choke or get fluid in its lungs.

If the additional body warmth and supplemental feedings work and the puppy seems to be returning to normal, place it back with its mother and observe whether she accepts it or not. If she accepts it, it may survive. If it is rejected and cast aside, you have little choice but to keep trying by using heating pads to keep it warm and supplemental feedings to keep it strong. The survival rate for such pups is low.

Hypoglycemia

Hypoglycemia—or low blood sugar—is a health problem that affects some Pomeranian puppies between five and 16 weeks of age and all Pom owners must be on the lookout for it. Hypoglycemia is recognizable by a healthy puppy suddenly becoming weak, listless, unaware of its surroundings, even unable to walk or stand. Advanced stages include seizures before lapsing into a coma, which is followed by death. Steps should be taken to immediately give the pup glucose or sugar. Karo syrup is an excellent, easy source to have on hand. Mixed with warm water and administered by eye dropper, it can save the puppy's life until veterinary help can be found. Some breeders also let an ill pup lick Nutra-Cal off their fingers if the dog is strong enough to do it. Nutra-Cal is a high caloric paste supplement that contains vitamins, fats, carbohydrates and proteins. Other breeders recommend "pediatric stat," a highly concentrated nutrient stress formula that contains the necessary electrolytes plus 15 other substances to provide a balanced liquid diet.

A veterinarian might want to administer glucose injections to the pup until the blood sugar is stabilized. The puppy should be

Giving the pup something to chew on will help strengthen its teeth and protect the furniture. *Welsh*

A puppy tired from playing and chewing will head for a basket and someone to curl up with.

Of course, some puppies, such as Ina
Kniffin's, would rather untie a bow.

134

Still others would rather explore pumpkins.

carefully watched thereafter. No one actually knows why Pomeranian puppies are particularly susceptible to hypoglycemia. Some breeders think it is due to nutrition and they advocate a natural, well balanced, raw diet, which is believed to keep the electrolyte level even throughout the puppy's growing period and extremely active life patterns. Others just take the precaution of giving their pups a daily sugar supplement. Whatever breeders do to handle the problem, they have a responsibility to advise all puppy buyers to be on the lookout for the slightest sign of low blood sugar reaction in the pup and give guidance on what should be done if it happens. Many breeders and many new Pomeranian owners have suffered heartache when their pup has been lost because of this deficiency.

Open Fontanelle

Open Fontanelle sometimes occurs in Pomeranians. Many small dogs, especially the diminutive ones, have soft spots on the tops of their heads that are never fully covered over by bone mass when the dog matures. In a tiny Pom, this soft spot feels like a little hole. If the hole is really small, the Pom should lead a normal life. However, if the skull opening is large the dog may have problems with normal growth and could develop seizures. Only time will tell whether or not the dog is adversely affected by the failure of the soft spot to close over.

Common Disorders in Puppies

Other possible puppy problems are fairly common in most breeds. These include bleeding in stool or urine, or bleeding from any part of the pup's body; refusing to eat; weight loss; puppy bloat; unquenchable thirst and/or frequent urination; coughing or nasal discharges; crying out in pain when picked up or touched; and unusual lumps or bumps anywhere on the pup's body. In all cases, the puppy should be taken at once to a veterinarian for diagnosis and treatment.

Not only illnesses demand veterinary assistance. Pomeranian teeth also need attention. At about three weeks of age, the first

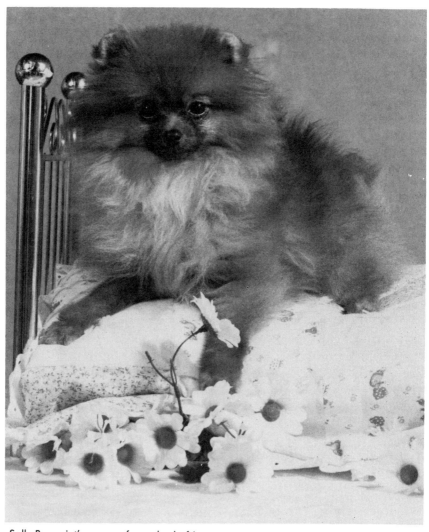

Sally Baugniet's pup prefers a bed of its own. *Paulette*

"milk" or "baby" teeth appear. Permanent teeth replace them when the pup is four to eight months old. Occasionally the permanent teeth will try to push through the gums before the baby teeth have fallen out. If this happens and a single tooth or double set of teeth begin to appear, the baby teeth should be removed. If the baby teeth are allowed to remain, misalignment of permanent teeth and a spoiled mouth could be the result. An adult Pom's teeth also need care. The teeth should be cleaned periodically and the Pom should be given safe chew bones or toys to strengthen and clean the teeth between regular cleanings.

New owners should carefully follow a breeder's advice on proper food, vaccinations and worming requirements for their puppy. All dog owners are advised to keep a dog health care medical book on hand for emergencies. A list of some excellent texts appears in the Appendix.

The American Pomeranian Club has been sponsoring national specialty shows since 1911. Judge at the 1964 event was Pom breeder Col. James K. Arima and the Best of Breed winner was Ch. Edward's Reddy Career, owned by Robwood Kennels. He was handled to this win by Joy S. Brewster. *Loconte*

Percy Roberts awarded a winners ribbon to Strait's Tiny Tim, handled by Frank Ashbey, during an outdoor national specialty show held in conjunction with a Westchester Kennel Club show. *Shafer*

16

Searching for a Pomeranian Puppy

WHETHER YOU ARE a breeder with a litter to sell, or a prospective buyer who has searched high and low for the perfect pet, the Pomeranian puppy is the focal point. A conscientious breeder wants to sell his or her puppy to the best home and a serious buyer wants to purchase a healthy, happy pup with whom to share a lifetime.

Every breeder has a right to ask a prospective buyer a myriad of questions concerning a potential buyer's background, dog knowledge, desires and intentions. A prospective buyer should be able to personally visit with the puppy that is for sale, see its dam, litter mates, if any, and discuss with the breeder the pup's health, shots and general care. It is expected that both the buyer and the seller would be wary of each other. They have a lot at stake, but it is the puppy itself that has the most to lose when it is being purchased by a buyer who is ill-equipped to care for it.

No one should ever buy a Pomeranian if they are not prepared to devote time, effort and money to the little dog's well-being. Not only must its health be carefully looked after and periodic shots and checkups attended to, but every degree of its life demands mindful attention. Is the animal being fed good dog food? Is the vitamin intake adequate? Is it being properly bathed and groomed? Are its home surroundings clean and pleasant? Does it have toys to play with? And, perhaps most important of all, are its human relationships fun, loving and plentiful? If the answers are negative in nature, then no Pomeranian—or any dog for that matter—should be owned by the individual seeking such animal. A dog demands companionship and will give companionship in return. It needs attention, and in return will be mindful. It seeks love, and will smother its owner with adoration. A dog is a wonderful creature, but it needs respect, care and love.

Anyone wishing to buy a Pomeranian, or who wants to learn more about the breed, should attend local dog shows. The American Kennel Club, 51 Madison Avenue, New York, New York 10010 may be contacted for information about all-breed kennel clubs in a given area. The AKC also has on hand a list of national and local breed clubs with secretaries' names and addresses whom can be called for breed and show information.

Armed with this data, a person interested in learning about Pomeranians should contact the club representatives and inquire as to local breeders and shows. Communicate with the breeders by letters or telephone and express interest in the breed. Do not just visit a kennel without first calling. No kennel owner appreciates or is likely to help someone who fails to exhibit common good manners.

Below is a list of the current Pomeranian associations and the regional territories they cover. Present club secretaries are not listed because they frequently change. A call of the AKC for the name and address of the current breed club secretaries will enable an interested buyer to contact that person for regional breed club activities and membership information.

The national breed club, which services a membership from around the country, is known as the American Pomeranian Club, Inc. There are 13 regional clubs:

Arizona	Pomeranian Club of Greater Phoenix
California	Northern California Pomeranian Club
	San Diego Pomeranian Club
	City of Angels Pomeranian Club
Hawaii	Pomeranian Club of Hawaii
Illinois	Western Pomeranian Club
	(covers the Midwest)
Iowa	Pomeranian Club of Greater Des Moines
Massachusetts	Bay Colony Pomeranian Club
Michigan	Pomeranian Club of Michigan
Oregon	Columbia Pomeranian Club
Texas	Dallas-Fort Worth Pomeranian Club
	Pomeranian Club of Greater Houston
Washington	Puget Sound Pomeranian Club

Several of the regional Pomeranian Clubs around the country hold their specialty shows in conjunction with all-breed shows. At a Bay Colony Specialty show, breeder-judge Mary S. Brewster awarded Best of Breed to Ina Kniffin with her Ch. Leader's Little Buck-A-Roo. Buck-A-Roo won the Toy Group at Westminster in 1967.   *Shafer*

All-breed shows are good forums for sharing dog experiences and ideas. The Westchester Kennel Club sponsors one of America's premier events every September. Show chairman Judson L. Streicher, left, holds one of the trophies, while judge Haworth F. Hoch awards the ribbon to Ch. Fun Fair Pinto O'Joe Dandy. Pinto was shown by Joy S. Brewster. The other trophy presenter is club president, A. Peter Knoop.   *Ashbey*

17

Grooming and Trimming

ALL LONG-COATED BREEDS need to be groomed to prevent matting of the hair and to reduce shedding. The Pomeranian, whether a pet or a show dog, is no different—it needs to be groomed. In fact, grooming or brushing is something that a Pom and its master should both look forward to giving and receiving. This is a good time for an owner to demonstrate love and special attention to the affectionate animal and such contact is a positive, private experience for the dog, who knows it is loved and being cared for.

The Grooming Routine

Pomeranian breeders begin grooming their dogs early in life, usually at three to four weeks of age. A soft brush is gently stroked against the natural lay of the hair to get the young pup used to being brushed. At first the dog is held in the breeder's lap, and later it can stand on a grooming table. The puppy learns that grooming can be fun. As the puppy matures, a stiffer brush is used and the dog becomes accustomed to lying on its side while its coat is carefully brushed from the skin outward and upward. Any mats are gently pulled apart and combed through with a smooth-tipped steel comb. Extra attention is paid to the coat when the pup begins to lose its puppy coat and the mature hairs set in. The coat will easily mat if this loose coat is not promptly removed.

Grooming Technique

Grooming an adult Pom that has been trained since it was young to enjoying the process of grooming is a pleasure for its owner. Chris Heartz, of Chriscendo Kennels, offers her grooming techniques:

> There is nothing more attractive than a Pom standing before you, his coat groomed to perfection, every hair gleaming and standing straight off from his body.
>
> To achieve this, the grooming equipment is minimal—a pin brush, slicker, comb, spray bottle of water mixed with 1 oz. of cream rinse, and baby powder or cornstarch for cleaning.
>
> Begin by brushing the chest coat. If your Pom doesn't lay on his back or side, it is best to put a towel on your lap as you sit in a chair. Most dogs will lay fairly quietly and endure the grooming.
>
> Starting with the tummy, you may find, if you are working on a male, the "underneath" slightly gummed-up. Spray fairly heavily and dry off with a towel. From the center of the stomach, working up the chest, parting the hair in layers of about 1″, brush downward from the skin out to the ends of the coat. Spray each layer of hair with a mist of the water/cream rinse mixture. At the same time, the legs can be brushed with a slicker, upward.
>
> Check to be sure you have brushed up the entire front leg and be sure there are no tangles behind the elbows, a place that mats quickly. Powder may be sprinkled over the tummy area to keep it fresh smelling and dry.
>
> The rest of the body coat is done with the dog lying on his side. Continue brushing in layers of about 1″ from the skin outward. Work in rows parallel to the backbone, brushing each layer which has been sprayed. A very thick coat may be brushed out with a slicker brush, carefully and slowly so as not to tear out the undercoat. These rows are not just in the center of the body, but start at the front of the chest or shoulder area all the way to the upper thigh area. Work carefully through the neck, ear area, carefully separating any tangles with your

A Pomeranian should always be brushed thoroughly and carefully. Chris Heartz's sketches demonstrate the proper direction for brushing.

Subtle roundness is a key feature to consider when grooming a Pom.

fingers and brushing with a slicker, if need be. Continue to the center of the back. Turn the dog over and repeat the procedure to the other side.

When both sides are thoroughly brushed out, stand the dog up on the table and holding the tail in one hand, spray and carefully brush in long strokes, being careful not to tear out any hair. Now brush all the coat forward from the head moving back to the tail and brushing forward.

Push all the chest hair up toward the head with your hand, take a 1″ layer starting between the legs and work up toward the chin in layers. On a puppy or a short coated dog you may want the coat to frame the face. In that case, brush a second time, starting at the chin. Brush each layer up towards the chin.

Set the dog on the table, let him shake and then mist the entire coat with the spray. Brush the front down, the body coat forward, the pants down and the tail out and forward towards the head.

The coat is now ready for the show ring, or for the bath.

Chris Heartz follows her grooming suggestions with some thoughts on trimming the Pomeranian for the show ring:

Begin by re-reading the article on grooming. To trim, you must have before you a clean Pom, brushed thoroughly through to the skin, every hair standing off from the body. Mist the coat lightly with water to achieve maximum fullness.

Begin trimming with the ears. Hold the ear leather between your thumb and forefinger, cover the tip of the ear with your thumbnail. With sharp scissors cut a straight cut across the top of each ear, at the level of the thumbnail. You may want to make two diagonal cuts on the outside of the ear to meet another cut on the inside. The cuts should not be any longer than 1/2″. Be careful not to make these cuts too long as it will make the ears appear larger. You want to achieve the illusion of tiny ears hidden in a ruff.

The head and ruff does not have to be trimmed unless the coat is very long and fine. Shortening this type of coat will make it appear more standoffish. Trim with shears and then re-trim with thinning scissors to avoid a "scissored" appearance.

Trimming the feet begins with short nails. The Canadian standard, as an illustration, calls for "small, compact feet," "standing well up on toes."

It is easier to start from birth rather than fight to get those "eagle talons" to resemble cat feet. Keeping the nails initially short far outweighs the extra effort, and the result is pretty feet with much less pain.

Begin by trimming all the hair between the pads. Trim very carefully, using small, blunt scissors. Large shears could easily seriously damage the tiny pads.

With a slicker brush, brush all the hair on the feet and legs upwards. Hold the foot out and trim neatly around the foot and up the leg. Don't stand the foot down on the table and trim around it without brushing upwards. The foot will not look like little "posts." The coat in front of the toes needs to stay as long as the toes to give the illusion of "no toes." Repeat the process with each leg.

Trimming the rear is done in stages. Beginning with the tail remember, *never shave the tail.* An exposed tail bone on a Pom is ugly. If there is an abundance of coat under the tail, it may help to run thinning scissors through the path where the tail lies to help it lie flatter. *Do not* scissor off the hair under the tail. A few judicious cuts with the thinning scissors will be fine. Remember though, if the dog has a poor tail set *nothing* will improve the way it lies.

The hair around the anus should be trimmed for both cleanliness and neatness. A circle about the size of a quarter will do.

Generally, the pants do not have to be trimmed. They are not attractive if they are cut squarely off. One thing to do is, when drying the coat, be sure to dry the pants *down* a layer at a time, starting at the hocks. This adds to the illusion of a shorter body. Pants that stick a way out behind and trail the ground like a Peke may tend to make the body look long. It is important that the Pom present the appearance of a compact, short-coupled dog. Trimming should always be for neatness and the Pom should never appear "scissored." Have someone move the dog after you make each alteration, work slowly and study what you have done.

Grooming and trimming the Pomeranian are not difficult, but many newcomers to the breed are unsure and apprehensive when they work with their dog, especially when they try trimming for the show ring. With this thought in mind, another excellent view on grooming and trimming is offered by long-time Pomeranian breeder, exhibitor and handler, Forrest McCoy:

Grooming the Pomeranian seems for some reason to be difficult for so many people. In reality, it is so very uncomplicated. Grooming a pet Pom or housedog, if you prefer, is quite simple.

The Pomeranian is a naturally clean dog. An occasional bath and a thorough brushing will keep him in excellent shape. Brushing to remove soil and prevent tangles and matting of the coat are most important. A good natural bristle brush is excellent for this. Be gentle and make it enjoyable for your dog. Teach him to stand on a table for his grooming. You will both enjoy it more this way. It is a perfect time to develop the relationship we all enjoy with our pets. Keep the nails trimmed to a comfortable length. Do not let them grow so long that you can hear them striking the floor when he walks. This is very painful for him. If you are unable or unwilling to cut the nails yourself, ask your veterinarian to do it for you.

Now, I would like to address myself to the serious exhibitor of Pomeranians: whether a breeder or one who has purchased a fine show specimen. What I am about to discuss comes from over 30 years of experience with the breed. Some breeders and exhibitors may find some of my grooming methods unconventional and debatable. However, the results and my record of presentation cannot be denied. During these years, along with my wife, Mary, I have been owner, breeder and exhibitor of Poms. I was a professional handler, and am presently approved by the AKC to judge Pomeranians along with other toy breeds.

I must repeat—grooming the Pom is not difficult. It is simply a matter of knowing the appearance you desire for your dog and practicing your technique until you obtain that end result. I am first going to list tools, supplies, etc., which I feel are necessary to keep a Pom groomed for showing.

1. Scissors—high quality, medium-size barber shears. At least two pair.
2. Brushes—high quality natural bristle. Two brushes.
3. Pin brush—medium size with "metal" (never plastic or nylon) pins.
4. Fine tooth comb—sometimes called a "flea comb."
5. Wide tooth comb—at least two.
6. Nail clippers—either scissor or guillotine type, your preference.
7. Emery boards—such as you use on your own nails.
8. Thinning shears—medium.
9. A "stone"—Marketed by Dr. Scholls, a "stone" is used to remove callouses from your own feet.
10. Medium grit sandpaper.
11. A good coat dressing in a spray bottle.

12. A heavy bath towel.

13. A bottle of Kwik Stop, Monsels or an ash tray full of cigarette ashes.

14. A good talcum powder or after shave powder.

15. Baby oil.

16. Elbow grease and perseverance.

Naturally, I am assuming you have a grooming table of some sort.

I realize that right now some of you are mystified by some of the items listed. Rest assured before you are finished you will find I have a use for each and every item.

I am going to assume you are grooming a mature, experienced dog. First off, let me say I am not going to bathe the dog. If there are any extremely dirty areas such as around the vent and the breeching, I will clean those areas with a wet wash cloth. I will wet the large bath towel in the hottest water I can stand to handle. Wring out as much water as possible. Wrap this around the dog, covering him completely except for his head. Hold him in your arms wrapped in this fashion for three to five minutes. I call this steaming a Pom. I learned this from an old-time breeder. Remove the towel and brush vigorously. Notice how you have removed the soil from the coat, and how the coat has opened up and come to life. We now have a clean dog with an open coat and are ready to start grooming. It is not necessary to steam your Pom each time you groom. Only when cleanliness dictates.

Stand your dog on the table facing you and start brushing just behind the ears. Remember everything brushes towards the head. At the base of the ears is a particularly oily spot. This is the place for your powder. Sprinkle powder liberally behind the ears and massage it into the coat with your fingers. With your pin brush remove the powder and you also remove the oil. Be alert for any mats which are starting to form. Separate them with your fingers and remove with the wide tooth comb. Back to using the pin brush, lifting, separating with a vigorous lifting motion. Remember, you are not raking leaves or chopping cotton. You are dressing a valuable canine asset. You must learn to cherish each hair as if it were gold. Sometimes I felt it would be easier to obtain gold than produce a fine show coat.

Continue brushing until you have covered the entire dog from front to rear. Don't forget to comb the feathering on the rear of the front legs. This is the place for the fine tooth "flea" comb. Endeavor to train this feathering to stand out straight towards the rear of the legs. Your dog should be completely dry now and the coat should be

150

standing. If not, liberally powder your dog all over and repeat, yes, repeat the procedure.

Now we are ready to do any trimming that is necessary. Don't be nervous as it is quite simple and if you mess it up, it will grow back in about three weeks.

We will start with the feet. I would advise you to look over a cat's foot. This is a good picture of what a Pom foot should look like when you are finished. One hard and fast rule to remember: we never trim anything from the top of the foot. I prefer to sit in a chair and lay my dog on his back on my legs with his head resting on my knees. He may object to this at first, but a little tummy scratching and sweet talk will restore his confidence. With the dog in this position, I trim the hair from the bottom of the feet and from between the toes and foot pads. It is very important for this hair to be removed. Failure to do so will allow it to become so dense it will spread the toes and your dog will appear splay footed. While the dog is in this position, this is also the best time to trim the back of the rear legs to the hock joint. Trim it quite close, but be careful not to nick the leg.

Having trimmed the bottom of the feet and the back of the rear legs, place your dog back on the table. Take a short break for yourself and your dog. Allow him to shake, and praise him for being good. Now, back to work.

With your dog standing on a smooth solid surface, take your scissors and trim around the edges of his feet. Be sure you are holding your scissors perpendicular to the surface he is standing on. If done with enough patience and pleasant conversation, the dog will soon learn to ignore what you are doing and will listen to your foolish ad lib. "Confidence."

Next, we will trim the dog's ears. I can hear the comments now, "Oh, my no. I can't. I will ruin him." Hogwash! If hands such as mine can accomplish this task, it should be simple for others. It is merely a matter of practice, patience and perseverance.

Place your dog on the table facing you, and I hope you are seated. This grooming can be a tiring, back breaker otherwise. Now is a good time to engage in a bit of foolish conversation with your dog. This will reassure him and gain his confidence. Using your pin brush and wide tooth comb, bring the hair around the ears up and forward. Get it standing up around the ears like a halo. Now, carefully and as gently as possible, grasp the leather of the ear firmly between the thumb and forefinger. Brush the long guard hairs back and away from the ears. As you are now holding the ear, the heel of your hand is against the side of his head. Your thumb is on the inside of the ear and the

A lot of people have difficulty trimming ears. A
proper trim is neat and barely detectable.

The ears should enhance the dog's facial features
and help symmetrically balance the head.

forefinger is curved behind the ear. With your thumbnail, locate the end of the ear leather. Protect the leather with your nail and very carefully make a straight, level cut across the tip of the ear. Make sure you have all the long guard hairs out of the way before making this initial cut. We only want to cut the short dense hair on the ear tip. Do not relax your grip on the ear. Using your thumbnail as a guide, trim the hair around the tip of the ear. This will necessitate your trimming down the sides of the ear for 1/4 to 3/8 of an inch.

Now release your grip and reassure your dog. Let him relax for awhile. Look over what you have done. I'm sure it looks rough and you are not happy with what you see. At least, I hope you are not.

Brush the ear up again and separate the guard hairs back out of the way. You must remove the blunt cut lines which you have created. This is where the sandpaper becomes important. Hold the ear between the thumb and forefinger as before, only this time the thumb and forefinger should be about halfway down the ear. Allow the upper portion of the ear to roll or lay back over your finger. This will expose the inner surface of the ear. Very gently and carefully rub the inner tip of the ear with sandpaper. Always stroke away from you. This will wear away the tips of this fine hair and eliminate the rough scissor line. To refine it even more, use the stone callous remover I recommended. Now brush all the hair up around the ear and look over your handiwork. I am sure you will be pleased. However, if you are not, then carefully repeat whatever step is necessary. Always remember if you cut very carefully, I mean maybe 1/16th of an inch at a time, you are much safer. You can always cut again and again, but only time and nature can replace it if you cut too much off.

Now that you have trimmed one ear, brush both ears forward, look them over and trim the second ear to match the one already done. It is best for this trimming to be done about ten days before the show date.

You now have one bit of trimming left—the nails. The nails must be kept as short as possible for the foot to retain its shape and be neat in appearance. I prefer to be seated and place the dog on my legs on his back with his head on my knees. You may use whatever type of nail trimmer you prefer. I have used both the guillotine and the scissor style with equal success. This is the time to have either Kwik Stop, Monsels Salts, or cigarette ashes handy. These are all effective coagulants in case you trim the nail too close. The cigarette ashes are the least effective but will do the job. If the nails are light in color your job is much easier. The "quick," or fleshy part of the nail, is readily visible in the light nail. You merely trim as close to it as possible. If you happen to nick the "quick" place some coagulant on it to stop the bleeding and continue. If your dog has dark or black nails, be very careful. It is impossible to see the quick on black nails. So you must trim very carefully a little at a time. By looking closely at the end of the freshly trimmed nail, you can tell when you are near to the quick. Stop just short of the quick and dress the nail with the emery board. If you trim often and file close to the quick, it will recede over a period of time. This will allow you to trim the nails even shorter. Even on black nails you will learn to recognize new growth and can trim accordingly.

Your dog is clean, trimmed and looking sharp, but you are not finished. Stand the dog on the table and spray him thoroughly with a good coat dressing. He should be just damp all over and not soaking wet. Brush him completely dry and get the hair standing on end all over. Take the baby oil and pour a few drops in the palm of your hand. Rub your hands together and apply this oil to the *tips* of the guard hairs. Do not rub it into the coat. We merely want to oil the *tips* of the long guard hair. This oil treatment will stop the breaking and splitting of the long hairs. Then they will reach their ultimate length. Leave this oil on your dog until the next grooming, which should take place within, at most, two days. When on a circuit of shows, I do not recommend oil between shows unless you have at least a one-day break between shows.

After the oil process, when you groom your dog the next time initially powder the dog all over. Then brush thoroughly. This will remove the oil. The only time you should ever brush a coat without spraying it first is when removing this oil. Brushing a dry coat will break and tear the guard hairs.

A few words concerning dogs who are blowing or shedding coat—when you notice the undercoat starting to loosen up, get it out of there. If left, it will only cause matting and delay the growth of the new coat. The sooner you remove the dead hair, the sooner you will have a beautiful new coat.

Grooming must be a continual process. Regardless of whether you are showing next week, next month or several months, you must continually cultivate your dog's coat. The idea that you can neglect your grooming until a few days before showing is ridiculous. This is a continual process. If you are not willing to make this amount of effort, I recommend a short haired breed for you.

Our own multi-Best in Show winner began her career at ten months of age, and won her last group at age eight years. During her show career, I can count on the fingers of one hand the number of times she missed more than two days being groomed completely. I might add that during this entire time, she never had a bath as such. She was cleaned by steaming, powder, coat dressing, brush and lots of elbow grease. The natural oils you wash out with repeated bathing cannot be replaced by any conditioners or substitute oils.

Good grooming is hard work, but most rewarding. A well-groomed Pomeranian is a thing of beauty which cannot be duplicated. Once you develop a routine, these grooming sessions become the most relaxing time of the day. This is when you develop the rapport between dog and master which is necessary in the show ring.

Trimming: How Much?

There is a lot of controversy about trimming the Pomeranian for the show ring. The standard clearly says that "trimming for neatness is permissible," and goes on to try to concisely define what is neat trimming around the feet, back of legs, edge of ears and around the anus. Some exhibitors and breeders, however, feel that neatness should also include stray hairs that detract from the pretty picture of a "rounded" Pom. This additional trimming, while against a strict interpretation of the breed standard, does enhance a dog's appearance as long as it is not overdone. Unfortunately, some overzealous exhibitors and handlers will actually use the scissors to "sculpt" the dog so that he appears to be what he is not. A tight coat (scissored short) will help to hide a breed incorrect soft outercoat; a well-trimmed tail (scissored short hairs on tail base, around anus and hip bones) may make a long-backed, low-tail set look better than it really is; a short bib (tightly scissored on an angle) can also shorten the dog's appearance. These are but a few of the ways to deceive through overscissoring. Too much scissoring should definitely not be permitted. However, slight trimming for tidiness, as opposed to sculpturing, helps present a "clean" looking Pom.

Many exhibiting Pom breeders have privately decided how to best handle this controversial question of the breed standard. Some trim for neatness and others overtrim in an effort to sculpture the dog's general appearance. Our judges, who are charged with interpreting the standard and applying the same against the dogs before them, have also had to find their personal solutions in how to handle this question. It is unfortunate that those who are guilty of

BEFORE

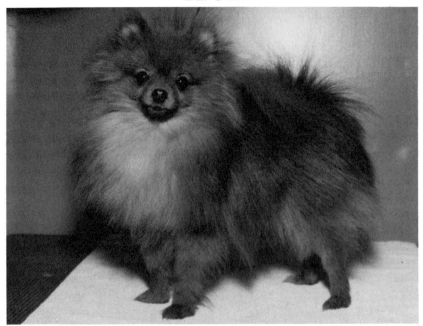

Sideview with the head facing forward. Stray hairs are going every which way around the head and long hairs on the feet make the dog's paws appear elongated. *Ashbey*

Sideview of an untrimmed Pomeranian. *Ashbey*

156

AFTER

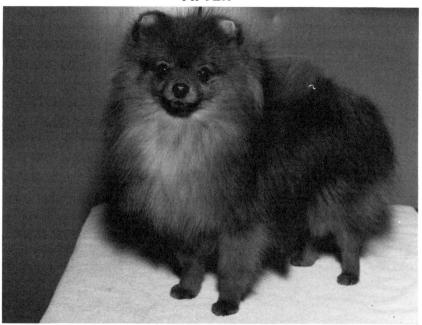

Sideview trimmed, dog facing camera. The stray hairs have been taken off, the ears gently pointed and excess hairs eliminated from the dog's paws. Hair has been carefully snipped from the base of the tail. The appearance is one of subtle "roundness." *Ashbey*

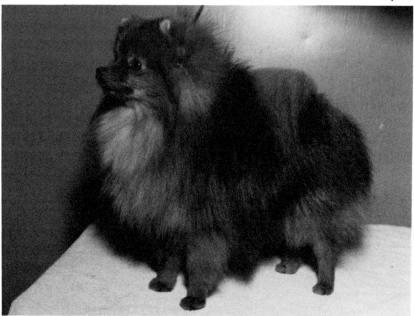

Sideview trimmed. *Ashbey*

The untrimmed head.   *Ashbey*

The trimmed head.   *Ashbey*

Which is more pleasing to the eye—a tidy dog or a scruffy one?

158

overtrimming manage to overshadow the topic of trimming for neatness and neatness alone.

Trimming is not an easy task for anyone. Newcomers approach it with trepidation, and experienced exhibitors and handlers either trim too little, too much or too obviously.

A good trim job blends in so that it is barely noticed. A bad job sticks out with sharp scissor lines and/or obvious sculpting. One person who is particularly talented with the scissors is Joy S. Brewster, a successful Pomeranian breeder and handler of many years. Joy can take an untrimmed dog and within a short period have him "cleaned-up" without sharp lines or conspicuous visual attempts aimed at altering the dog. She says all you need is "patience, a good eye and lots of practice."

A show dog needs to feel it is beautiful. *Ashbey*

160

18

Showing Your Pomeranian

LET US ASSUME you have purchased a show-quality Pomeranian puppy from a recognized kennel. You would like to train your pup for the show ring, but know absolutely nothing about dog shows.

The first step would be to attend a local all-breed dog show. To find out when such an event is scheduled for your area, contact the American Kennel Club for information about local all-breed clubs. Inquire from the club secretary as to the date of the next show and when you could call again to find out about the scheduled time for Pomeranian judging. While attending the show watch the Poms being judged, talk with exhibitors, and stay around to observe other breeds and take in the flavor of a dog show.

In the meantime, visit libraries and bookstores and read as much as possible about dog shows. A list of recommended reading material appears in the Appendix.

Not only is it necessary for you to learn about dog shows

through reading and observing, but your puppy should also be trained for its eventual first steps in the conformation ring. Local handling classes sponsored by kennel clubs are a great way for both of you to get some practical show experience. Talk with nearby breeders and handlers and ask for assistance. Try to get an honest evaluation of your dog's breed quality and learn how to present it to its best advantage.

Not all dogs take to dog shows. Some absolutely hate them, others tolerate them and others cherish the experience. Those who fall in the latter category and have good breed quality will become great show dogs. Great show dogs are not just born—they are worked with, fussed over and treasured. Some suggestions for training that great show dog of the future are offered by Susan Heckmann Buckel, daughter of the late, noted Pomeranian handler and all-breed judge, Winifred Heckmann. Susan has also successfully piloted many Pomeranians to Best in Show and specialty wins.

The first and most important element in making a Pom a great show dog is understanding its temperament. Through the years of campaigning a number of top-winning dogs and bitches, I have noticed that the majority of breeders and owners have an alarming tendency to raise the breed as tiny, fragile lap dogs, which, of course, is not at all consistent with the breed's actual disposition. Originally, the Pomeranian was a much larger dog than those seen today and although the breed size has diminished, the size of their hearts and their incredible fortitude has remained unchanged. As a result, the Pom is one of the biggest little breeds in dogdom. I have found the breed to be fearless, aggressive and strong-willed and, if raised properly, these little dogs will really own the ground they walk on.

The second most important element in raising a great show dog is realizing that you are dealing with a breed which is remarkably intelligent. Pomeranians have a rather uncanny and sometimes unnerving ability to understand you better than you do! They are characteristically almost cat-like for they are independent, inquisitive and very outgoing. However, at the same time, the breed is extremely affectionate and loving. It's understandable that we are inclined to want to spoil them. I cannot stress enough the importance of building a special rapport between yourself and your Pom—it is absolutely essential. A lot of this can be achieved through eye contact. In those few intimate moments, staring eye-to-eye with your little dog, it should feel as though he were trying to become part of you and you part of him. This creates a feeling of mutual respect and understanding and if you are successful in establishing such a relationship your dog will never take his eyes off you.

Now, how do we incorporate the above into that special puppy—that pick of the litter—that great show dog to be?

First, after the puppies have been weaned from the bitch, separate the litter and give each pup a stuffed toy. These toys will become your dog's friend and constant companion when you are not around. Every dog I've shown has gone home with a toy and still to this day that toy is his or her best friend. From this stage up until three months physical contact is very important. Spend time hand feeding, talking, cuddling and playing with your puppy. Play time should also include the stuffed toy (remember, best friend). Also encourage strangers to pick up and play with your puppy.

Puppies should be raised in a house environment, preferably in a place where they will be exposed to a lot of noise and commotion. A place like the kitchen with pots banging and children yelling is a good example. This setting is ideal to help build security for your puppy and prepare him for the excitement and noisy distractions of a dog show.

At three months of age, puppies should be broken on a tight lead. Teach him to pull on the lead so that he will learn how to move out on the lead—pulling you. This can be accomplished very easily by allowing him to chase a dog in front of him or by throwing a toy or tidbit. The Pomeranian is a breed which must exhibit great confidence on the ground. Therefore, this time is extremely important in its development as a show dog. Practice setting your puppy up and having people go over him so he gets used to people coming down on him. For a little dog accustomed to viewing the world at ground level, it's important that he finds human friends with a soft touch coming from the sky. Hand contact is absolutely essential at this point. From a gentle stroke or reassuring pat, your dog will gain much needed security and eventually will be able to wean himself from you, coming into his own state of confidence and independence.

Don't forget that although working with your puppy on the ground is extremely important, training and acclimating him to a table cannot be overlooked. Allow him to get used to the difference in height by picking him up and carrying him in your arms. The puppy should be groomed on the table and, once again, people should examine him and go over everything, including his bite. Please—one

A Pomeranian puppy will love the fuss and attention it gets during its training for the show ring.

"A Pomeranian should not be treated like a porcelain statue or Dresden doll." *Ashbey*

piece of advice I strongly urge you to follow is that when your dog is on the table never, and I mean not for one split second, take your hands off him. If a Pom were to fall off a grooming table, it would be equal to either you or I falling off the Empire State Building.

When preparing to exhibit your puppy, first take him to several shows but don't show him. Allow a few weekends of spending time in an exercise pen, indoors, up on your lap, etc., for him to familiarize himself with these new surroundings. Amazing as it seems, since most Poms are raised as hothouse plants, outdoor shows tend to be more frightening and intimidating than indoor ones. In either case, you must give him time to get used to this different environment. You will probably find that because the breed is so intelligent, your puppy will observe, listen and build self-assurance and confidence on his own.

Mind you, all of the above I would try to accomplish before the puppy is 12 months old. It's a fascinating observation and you won't want to hear it; however, between the age of 12 to 16 months, I would definitely keep puppies out of shows and take them back home to grow up. This is a stage in their maturing process in which they become very susceptible to noises and situations that for some reason they cannot cope with. Growing pains and chemical changes which are normal during this time in their development make all previous learning experiences secondary. So, show your puppy prior to 12 months of age, and put him away for the next four to six months. Believe it or not, you will really be ahead of the game.

Another important observation I would like to make is that God made Poms a hairy breed for a reason. Some of the problems in the breed today can be directly attributed to the fact that many breeders raise their dogs as hothouse plants. Actually they are much better off if they are allowed to be exposed to the elements of nature, of course in moderation. Pomeranians have a hardier constitution than appearances would suggest and therefore are more than quite capable and are much healthier if they can spend several hours outside a day. Everything in nature, again in moderation, is beneficial. Both the cold and rain are wonderful for the coat. Hot weather not only helps conditioning and endurance, but also is instrumental in keeping them in hair all year around. Fresh air, which is absolutely essential, can keep a breed which is subject to lung difficulties problem free. Last, but certainly not least, the sun. Poms, having for the most part been raised indoors, have a very hard time adjusting to light. Even indoors, I would suggest raising a litter in the brightest area possible. Darkness will only contribute to later on eye problems.

Dog shows can get boring, so it is important to take time to play with the show dog and let it know it is loved and appreciated.

Finally, the secret to molding a puppy into a great show dog is all the attention it receives on the road. Some dogs take a few months to make sense of this and others as long as a year. However, have patience because I've never had it fail.

Another secret of showing your puppy is that at whatever age you begin—remember always to make a firm understanding in the ring and on the road—from the beginning do not treat him as a porcelain statue or Dresden doll. Have fun! Play with your puppy. Talk to him, entertain him and the rewards of your efforts will be endless.

Lastly, if you start losing him—and I don't mean running out of the ring, but rather a sudden noise or distraction startles or frightens him—a familiar voice, his friendly toy, or a reassuring touch will rebuild his confidence and security.

If he looks forward to weekends of fun and entertainment, no matter what you look like you will have a real show dog at the other end of your lead.

Conformation showing is not for everyone, nor for every pure-bred dog. Some people walk away from a show thoroughly disgusted because "they" did not win. Others say everything is "fixed." But a great many people attend shows because they enjoy the experience. These are individuals who have come to terms with the fact that the judging of the dog and its competition is highly subjective and based on the personal opinion of the judge—an opinion that involves interpretative study of the breed standard, condition and showmanship of the dogs presented in the ring, and then a mental balance of one imperfect animal against another.

No dog show exhibitor should ever take a win or loss personally, nor should any dog ever mean more or less simply because it does or does not capture the ribbons at the show. A dog show should be regarded as an opportunity to share good times and conversation with other like-minded individuals and not just a vehicle for ego winning. Go to shows, have fun and enjoy your Pomeranian with others!

A portrait of Ch. Rider's Sparklin' Gold Nugget, owned by Mr. and Mrs. Porter Washington, bred by Blanche Rider, and shown by Porter Washington. Sparky was campaigned for approximately three years. During that time, he captured 159 Bests of Breed, 119 Toy Groups, and 41 Bests in Show. *Painting by Cleanthe*

Sparky taking Best in Show at San Gabriel.
Ludwig

19

Sparky's Story

S HOWING DOGS IS NOT EASY. A fantastic quality dog may not like to show, or a dog who really enjoys the shows may not possess enough positive breed characteristics to make it a great show dog. Any person who has a Pomeranian that has both excellent quality and the desire to show is very fortunate. One such dog was Ch. Rider's Sparklin' Gold Nugget, owned by Mr. and Mrs. Porter Washington of California and bred by Lee Johnson. During his show career, Sparky had won 41 all-breed Bests in Show, 119 Toy Groups and 159 Bests of Breed—a record that still holds to this date. Sparky's show path was not always an easy one, as demonstrated in this account of some highlights of his career written by his owner and handler, Porter Washington:

Sparky was a dog for all judges. He came to us by a stroke of luck, one might say, as Dicky (Mrs. Porter Washington) and I had just returned home from Westminster where our great Keeshond, Eng., Am. and Can. Ch. Wrocky of Wistonia, was beaten in the breed for the only time in his life, and we were rather sad.

It was early Sunday morning and a call came from Bert Heath, the then owner and publisher of *Kennel Review* magazine, saying he

169

had seen the best Pomeranian he had ever imagined. He went on to state that the dog, a seven-month-old puppy, had gone Best of Breed the day before under the famous Pom breeder, Mrs. Sally Cohen (Golden Glow Kennels) at the Pomeranian specialty. He also said he thought the dog would probably win the Toy Group at the Silver Bay Kennel Club show that day. He informed me that Mrs. Cohen and several well-known handlers were trying to buy the dog from its owner, Mrs. Blanche Rider. I asked what the highest offer was and he said $500, which was quite a sum for a seven-month-old puppy in those days. I told him to offer Mrs. Rider $750, and call me back.

In less than 30 minutes, the telephone rang and when I answered Bert said, "Brother, you've got a Pom." I yelled to Dicky and she came into the den with tears in her eyes. Our terrible disappointment at Westminster went out the window.

Bert told me he would call immediately after the Toy Group, so we sat down, relaxed and waited for his call. About seven that evening, the phone rang and it was Bert. He was laughing like a crazy man. He said the dog had won the Toy Group, picked up five additional points, giving him a total of ten in just two days. I told him that we would wait up until he got to our home. About 11:00 P.M., Bert and Bob Zacho, a handler friend, walked into the library with a toy crate. Bert put it down on the floor, opened the door and out walked the top-winning Pom that has ever lived.

At first he looked things over, sniffing the air and then went straight to Dicky. This was the beginning of one of the happiest experiences of our lives.

Back in those days it was possible to enter shows only one week prior to the show, so early Monday morning I rushed down to the Bradshaw office [the superintendent] and entered Sparky in Open Dogs at both Phoenix and Tucson for the following weekend. By the time we got to Phoenix, word was out. Needless to say Sparky took the breed both days. In just this short one week's time, he acquired enough points and majors to become a champion.

The rest of the Sparky story is legendary, but in the following paragraphs I will try and relate some of the highlights of his show career from my memory.

At that time, there were only about 20 or 25 shows a year on the West Coast. Handlers had to travel with full strings of dogs to the Pacific Northwest, Colorado, New Mexico, Arizona and Texas circuits to make it possible to compete for any national awards, such as the Quaker Oats Awards. Also, most of the handlers carried several group-quality dogs in their strings, as flying from place to place with one dog, as is now sometimes done, was unheard of back then. You just traveled from place to place and took your chances.

By the time Sparky was one year old, he was the top dog in my string, winning Toy Groups and always a strong contender for Best in Show. Anyone who saw Sparky could attest that he was all show dog. His movement was indescribable, and he never gave up no matter how hot or inclement the weather might be. He was himself inside and out.

Once at New Orleans on the Deep South circuit, the groups were being held indoors and it was very hot. Some of the top toys in America were in the group, including E. W. Tipton's famous Min Pin—Little Daddy, the Levy's Toy Poodle out of Miami and the great Peke—Chik T'Sun. It was thought by most that the Peke would get the nod, but I knew that before the judge handed out the ribbons he was going to see a show.

After examining the dogs and moving and moving and moving, the judge sent the Min Pin to the 3rd marker and the Toy Poodle to 4th. He then brought out the Pom and the Peke to let them move again. This was a mistake for the longer the two dogs moved in that heat the better Sparky became. The poor Peke was in trouble due to the heat. But it was to be just one of those days, the Peke won and Sparky was second. The late John Cuneo was on the slate that day and I saw him shake his head when we went to the numbers. Oh, well! You just can't win 'em all!

Three weeks later, Mr. Cuneo was to judge Best in Show at the San Gabriel Kennel Club show in Monrovia, California. The groups were being held outdoors in rather high grass. Sparky had won the Toy Group and when we went in for B.I.S., I took him to the rear of the line. Mr. Cuneo came back to me and said, "Bring that Pom up here." He took me to the head of the line-up, took one more look at the dogs and said, "Take 'em around." Sparky took off like he had been shot from a gun, and as I looked back while making the first turn, I saw that we were gaining on the Pointer, which was in back of us. Sparky was literally unbelievable. He would move out ahead of everything and keep going. Needless to say, he took Best in Show at San Gabriel that day.

Another happening that is indelible in my memory occurred at one of Golden Gate's winter shows held in the old auditorium. The late Louis Murr was to judge the Toy Group and the ring was a long one, with a mat down the center from end to end. When I came to move Sparky, Mr. Murr said to me, "Let him out as hard as he can go." I dropped the lead and said, "Come on, baby," and away we went. People in the balcony began stomping on the floor and whistling. I saw one hat go into the air. We took the group and when we came back in for the final, the crowd began to clap and yell when we came into the ring.

What you are about to read is something that I will never forget as long as I live.

Mrs. Mildred Imrie was to do the Best in Show honors, and after she had examined all six dogs, she started to move them. Sparky was the last dog to move, and when I brought him up to her she said, "Porter, just take him down about half way." I then answered by saying, "Why can't he go like the big dogs?" She remarked, "As you wish." Well, away we went full bore with the crowd going wild. I took him the full length of the ring and when I got back to Mrs. Imrie, she said, "Can he do it again?" I turned him and away we went again the full length of the ring. On the way back, half way down the mat, Mrs. Imrie held her hand in the air and said, "Best in Show."

Another show experience that shows what a great show dog Sparky was occurred just before the Tacoma Kennel Club show. At that time, Tacoma had put up a challenge trophy to be won three times by the same owner for permanent possession. We had won the first leg the previous year with our Kees, Wrocky.

Dicky and I discussed going up for the coming Tacoma Show, but it was hunting season and I wanted to go up to the Yakima Indian reservation for some pheasant shooting with an old friend, Vance McGilbry. Finally, we decided that I would drive up to Washington with my two Pointers—a bitch, Sheba, and a young dog, Winchester. Dicky would fly up and I would meet her on Thursday prior to the Sunday show. She arrived late in the evening. The next morning I arose early to take the dogs out for exercise. I drove out to the port of Tacoma and found a good spot away from any traffic, let down the tail gate of the station wagon and let both Pointers out. Off they went and were soon out of sight. I then turned Sparky out and proceeded to clean out the crates.

Without warning, Winchester came back to the car and the next thing I heard was a loud scream from Sparky. When I looked to see what had happened, around the car came Winchester with Sparky in his mouth. He was having a ball retrieving that Pom. I yelled at him to no avail, but he just kept on playing his game. Finally, I picked up a handful of gravel and threw it at the dog. Winchester then dropped Sparky, who at once ran under the car. He was still screaming when I crawled under to fetch him. I checked for tooth marks and was very relieved there were none. Winchester was a soft-mouthed dog, thank God!

Ch. Rider's Sparklin' Gold Nugget, 1954-1971.   *Tauskey*

Sparky taking Best in Show at Golden Gate the "night he tore the house down."

When I got back to the hotel, I told Dicky what had happened and asked her to come down to try and console the poor little dog. This she did and when she put a lead on Sparky he showed absolutely no interest. His tail was down and he was very cowered. Later that day we went to a park and tried again to get his attention, but there were no signs of improvement. We discussed whether we should start home and decided to wait. We took him into our room where he stayed all day Saturday and by Sunday morning he was starting to come around. Since Poms would not be judged until late Sunday afternoon, we decided to wait and see.

Sunday morning, I took Sparky for a walk down the street and although he showed no signs of happiness, he did come along with me. We went out to the show building after lunch and I told Dicky to get a catalog and locate the ring while I did up the dog. I brushed him out as usual, cut his nails and trimmed him on the legs. Then I put a toy lead on him and put him down. His tail went up and away we went. By the time his turn came to go in the ring, he was his old self.

Yes, we went Best in Show, got the second leg on that trophy and retired it the following year with my Beagle bitch, Ch. Sogo Won't Do It, making it three straight with three different dogs.

In closing, let me say that during my span of life in dogs, I have seen and shown many good ones and some great ones, but as long as I am on this Earth I shall never see another as great as Sparky!

20
Obedience Competition

IF YOU DISCOVER that your dog does not possess enough breed quality in comparison to the standard to show it in the conformation ring, or if you would like to be able to train your Pom for obedience competition or would like to explore both obedience and conformation, you would be advised to read some of the many excellent obedience books currently available. The Appendix lists several for your consideration.

Pomeranians are a unique breed and need special attention over and above those suggested in general obedience books. Two successful Pom breeders and exhibitors, who have also excelled in the obedience ring, are Jessie and Barbara Young of Jabil Kennels in New Hampshire. This is the advice they offer:

> You have only to look into the eyes of a Pomeranian to see that this is a bright, highly intelligent breed. Past generations of working and herding ancestors have left their mark on the working capabilities of Poms. You might notice that your Pom puppy, while still very young, "herds" you throughout the house. Some Poms go as far as to grab a portion of their "object's" pant legs, just as larger herding dogs do when they herd livestock. Poms also love to learn to retrieve toys and

other objects. These tendencies make Pomeranians "naturals" for obedience training. Their bouncy quick movements make them real crowd pleasers at obedience trials.

Obedience training gives you and your dog a chance for regular periods spent one-on-one with each other. It gives both you and your dog skills that are useful every day. It is not uncommon for owners of their first Pomeranian (or any Toy breed) to become a doting parent, carrying their dog instead of walking it on a leash. By the time the puppy matures physically and mentally, it is thoroughly territorial, and will growl or even snap if a stranger approaches its owner. This problem need never happen if the owner has the foresight to properly train and socialize the puppy.

There are many books available concerning obedience training, and dozens of different methods suggested. The important thing to remember is that, with all Toy breeds, you must scale your training down to fit the dog. The heavy snaps on most leashes are totally wrong for Poms, as are most training collars. There are lightweight nylon and jeweler's link chain "choke" collars available from pet suppliers, which fit easily into the coat and do not hang on the neck. A heavy collar, or one which is too long for the dog, interferes with the dog's movement and the dog will rebel against it. The leash should also be light and the clasp small. I have made my own by using six-foot boot laces, sewn to as lightweight a clasp as I can find. Sporting goods stores carry fishing tackle which is easily adapted for obedience work, with a swivel and safety pin-type hook.

Whether you want to train for AKC obedience titles, or simply want to learn a skill with your dog and increase the bond between you, it is a good idea to enroll in an obedience class. While there are kennels which will board your dog for a few weeks and train it for you, they usually cater to larger dogs and are not necessary for Poms. It is especially important if this is your first dog that you and your dog learn together, and you learn how your dog's mind works. There are many obedience training clubs throughout the country, as well as all-breed clubs and private individuals who have organized lessons.

You should investigate several such classes before you decide which class is right for you. You will be extremely fortunate if you can find a trainer who has had first-hand experience in training Toy dogs, as there are many differences between training a Border Collie or a Rottweiler and training a Pom or another Toy dog. An instructor who has personally worked with a small dog will be more empathetic to your needs, and will be able to share this experience with you.

One word of warning: in training my own Poms I have had two

"close calls" with larger dogs in class. You must be alert to the dogs around you, regardless of their size. If you feel uncomfortable near a particular dog, speak up. Even the best instructor may not be aware of a potential problem until it is too late, so be responsible for your friend.

If you want an obedient housepet, and have no intention of going on to competition, you can apply the skills you learn in class to your daily life. Grooming your Pom is so much easier if he knows Sit, Stand and Down. I guarantee you will draw comments from passersby if you and your dog are out walking (heeling) in public, with your Pom smartly at your left side. (You must also be cautious about unfriendly dogs in public.) Your veterinarian will love your Pom even more if he can sit or stand quietly on the examination table.

If you wish to train your Pom for competition, you have a marvelous, exciting challenge ahead. Pomeranians are generally high scoring workers, and I have never seen a Pom who did not enjoy showing off. However, you must keep in mind that your training must be geared to the Toy dog. You may be the only person with a Toy dog in your class, so you must take the things you learn from watching other people work and scale them down to fit your dog.

In heeling, you *must* remember that the Pomeranian's neck is short and his trachea is small. Every motion you make with the lead must be given with restraint. The length of your stride while heeling must be adapted to suit the pace of your Pom. Pomeranians can trot at a swift pace, but you must take shorter steps as you walk to make his work easier.

I have found that one of the most important tools that you can use in your training is your voice. You want your Pom to work in a happy way, so keep your tone light and encourage him. Always praise after each lesson.

And remember that, just as every person cannot become a star athlete or scholar, every dog cannot achieve a perfect score. When you and your dog have trained hard and you enter trials, do your best and be proud of your dog. Chances are that you will make more mistakes than your dogs, and there are always more trials you can enter.

If you decide to go on to more advanced work, including jumping, you must also condition your Pom physically before you begin to teach the jumping exercises. While the AKC standard for the Pomeranian calls for a short back, the breed is still expected to jump 1½ times its height on the high jump. And the truth is that some Poms are just not built to do this. If you have any question regarding your

"Cupid" performs a drop on recall.

"Roxy" displays Utility scent discrimination by selecting her object.

Gladys Dykstra's Pomeranians are lined up in a row waiting their instructions.

She retrieves over the high jump.

178

Another Pom that enjoys the jump is "Morris," owned by Rosalind Goltz.

Am. and Can. Ch. Topaze Lady Jennifer, Am. and Can. CDX, owned by Mary Casey and Gladys Dykstra, flies over the broad jump.

Cassio's Quarter Note, CD, owned by Rosalind Goltz, has a firm hold on his dumbbell.

Pom's physical ability, discuss it with your trainer and your veterinarian. If your Pom is too young, or if he is prone to loose stifles, you will have to forego jumping. In the case of a young dog, he should not jump before he is a year old, and after that time should be brought along slowly, as his conditioning increases. A dog with weak stifles should never jump, as it will only increase the problem. An extremely short-backed Pom will have a very difficult time working his way up to the proper height for competition. If your Pom is fine-boned, be very careful to jump only on a cushioned surface, never on cement, as the stress on the front legs during landing may be too much for fine bones.

Finally, you must know the lessons well and the requirements for each lesson before you start to instruct your Pom. He cannot be expected to learn if you do not know how to teach him.

Ch. Midas Touch of Serenity, owned by Jon and Roberta Massey, loves to lie on the bed surrounded by her stuffed toys.

21

Your Pomeranian Pet

A POMERANIAN NEED NOT be a show dog or even an obedience titlist to be enjoyed, because the Pom is a wonderful, loving pet that could not care less about titles. A quick-witted watchdog, a playful animal, a comforting companion—the Pomeranian is all of these. It adores children who will play with it; it is partial to the elderly who will comfort it. In short, the Pomeranian is delightful company for persons of all ages. Life is never boring or quiet when there is a Pomeranian around the house.

A Pom is a domesticated dog who needs to be kept clean, healthy and happy. For this reason, no Pom should ever be ignored or neglected. It is a wise owner who has armed himself with as much knowledge as possible about this unique breed. Such knowledge is not only garnered through books and periodicals, but also through direct contact with informed breeders. Any question, problem or difficulty should be immediately explored for possible solutions before the matter gets out of hand and the little dog pays an unnecessary price.

Breeders are the backbone of any breed. They readily share their experiences and wisdom with those who are willing to learn.

Marian Wingers says of Tamera, who was eight years old when she elected to take over the director's chair, "Her inner beauty matches her outer beauty."

Jabil's Petite Delilah, CD, at 16 years of age, chose to rest in a cushioned basket with two stuffed bunnies.

No owner of "just a pet" Pomeranian should be afraid to contact a breeder when a problem arises—or even with a seemingly simple question. Dog people will give of themselves to help others who are sincerely interested in dogs. They are a ready source to be tapped for assistance and information. Anyone who fails to make use of this help is letting down his pet in the process. Not only should one always strive to buy from a breeder, but one should also freely tap that eager source of information and guidance.

One such long-time breeder, Ina Kniffin of Tiny Tykes Kennel in New York, reports:

> Poms are the greatest dogs to live with. They are devoted and loving without being clingy. They are bold and brassy with strangers, and incomparable watch dogs. When I cry, they gather around to comfort me, pushing under my arms and licking my face. Poms can express total outrage when insulted or slighted. They will stomp off in a huff and sulk, but soon return to accept your apology and be pals again. Poms will listen attentively when you talk to them and seem to understand. They are the best company!

Another breeder, Olga Baker of Jeribeth Kennels in Texas, believes that Poms "are the silliest, cockiest, most enchanting creatures in the world. They flit around, learn about their world, eat voraciously and look, for all the world, like tiny wind-up toys."

One does not have to be a breeder to enjoy a beautiful Pom. Pomeranians adapt to all people—rich, poor, young, old, smart or otherwise. Everyone and anyone who think they own a Pom will soon learn that the Pom, in fact, owns them.

"The End"   *Brenda Thomson*

APPENDIX

International Pomeranian Standards

THE POMERANIAN CLUB STANDARD (ENGLAND)

General Appearance—Compact, short coupled dog, well knit in frame. Exhibiting great intelligence in expression; activity and buoyancy in deportment.

Characteristics—Sound, vivacious and dainty.

Temperament—Extrovert, lively and intelligent.

Head and Skull—Head and nose foxy in outline, skull slightly flat, large in proportion to muzzle which finishes finely and free from lippiness. Nose black in white, orange and shaded sable dogs; brown in chocolate tipped sable dogs, but in other colours may be "self-coloured," never parti-coloured or flesh.

Eyes—Medium size, slightly oval, not full, not set too wide apart; bright, dark and showing great intelligence. In white, orange, shaded sable and cream dogs, rims black.

Ears—Small, not set too wide apart, not too low down, but carried perfectly erect.

Mouth—Jaws strong, with a perfect, regular and complete scissor bite, i.e. the upper teeth closely overlapping the lower teeth and set square to the jaws.

Neck—Rather short and well set into shoulders.

Forequarters—Shoulders clean and well laid back. Fine boned legs, perfectly straight, or medium length in due proportion to size of dog.

Body—Back short, body compact, well ribbed up, barrel well rounded. Chest fairly deep, not too wide but in proportion to size of dog.

Hindquarters—Fine boned, legs neither cow-hocked nor wide behind; medium angulation.

Feet—Small, compact and cat-like.

Tail—Characteristic of breed high set, turned over back and carried flat and straight, profusely covered with long, harsh, spreading hair.

Gait/Movement—Free moving, brisk and buoyant.

Coat—Two coats, an under coat and an outer coat. Former soft, fluffy, the latter long, perfectly straight, harsh in texture and covering whole of body; very abundant round neck and fore part of shoulders and chest; forming frill extending over shoulders. Forequarters well feathered, thighs and hindlegs well feathered to hocks.

Colours—All colours permissible, but free from black or white shadings. Whole colours are: White, black, brown, light or dark, blue as pale as possible. Orange which should be self-coloured and bright as possible. Beaver. Cream dogs have black noses and black eye rims round eyes. Whites must be quite free from lemon or any other colour. A few white hairs, in any of the self-coloured dogs permissible but undesirable. Dogs (other than white) with white or tan markings highly undesirable and not considered whole-coloured specimens. In parti-coloured dogs, colours evenly distributed in body in patches; a dog with white or tan feet or chest not a parti-coloured dog. Shaded sables should be shaded throughout with three or more colours, the hair to be as uniformly shaded as possible,

188

and with no patches of self colour. In mixed classes, where whole coloured and parti-coloured Pomeranians compete together, the preference should, if all other points they are equal, be given to the whole-coloured specimens.

Size—Ideal weight, Dogs 1.8-2 Kg. (4-4½ lbs.); Bitches 2-2.5 Kg. (4½-5½ lbs.).

Faults—Any departure from the foregoing points should be considered a fault and the seriousness with which the fault should be regarded should be in exact proportion to its degree.

Note—Male animals should have two apparently normal testicles fully descended into the scrotum.

F.C.I. POMERANIAN STANDARD (Small Varieties)

Appearance—Small, elegant, quick, agile, nimble and dexterous in movement.

Head—Medium-sized; seen from above the head narrows wedge shaped to the point of the nose; seen from aside a moderate stop should be observed; the muzzle is not too long, and its length must show a balanced, proportional relationship to the forehead and the upper portion of the head; Nose is round and small; pigmentation on nose and around eyes and lips must be pure jet black on dogs with black, white, red-orange red or wolf-gray coats; chocolate colored dogs must have dark brown pigmentation on the nose and around the lips and eye rims.

Eyes—Dark, medium-sized, almond shaped and slightly slanted.

Ears—Ears are small and close together, triangular and erect; should not fall forward.

Neck—Medium in length; covered with profuse mane-like coat.

Body—Deep brisket; well-rounded ribs; straight, short back; tucked-up belly.

Tail—Set high, medium in length; must lie flat on the back from the root; may curve at the tip forming a roll or ring but must lie on the back and not the sides.

Legs—Medium in length, powerful, straight; hind-legs may be slightly angular at the hocks.

Feet—Small as possible; rounded with arched toes; so-called "cat-feet."

Coat—Short and dense on the head, ears, legs and feet; rest of body is profusely coated with long coat of stand-off texture; around the neck the hair is thickest and most profuse and should stand-off loose and straight from the body, without being wavy, curly or rough; on the back the coat may not part, but must stand off to all sides; the backsides of the front legs should be feathered profusely to the lower foreleg joint; on the hindlegs, the coat does not reach the hocks.

Colors—Black, white, dark chocolate, red-orange or red, wolf-gray. The smallest variety, which corresponds to the American or British Pomeranians weighing 5 pounds or less, may have other colors: blue, cream, beaver, parti-color. Parti-colors must have black, chocolate, gray or red-orange patches evenly distributed over the body.

Sizes—For the two smaller varieties: the smallest is a dwarf of 22 cm. in height or less at withers (under 9 inches) and corresponds to the smaller British and American Pomeranians, i.e. those weighing 5 pounds or less; the next size is called small, which measured at the withers 23-28 cm. (9 to 11 inches) and corresponds to the larger British and American Pomeranians, i.e. those weighing over 5 pounds.

Faults—Flat head; domed "apple-shaped" head; eyes too large; eyes too lightly pigmented; bulging "pop-eyes"; ears too long or set too widely apart; floppy ears not held erectly; flesh-colored nose, eye rims or lips; tail which is too short or does not lie firmly on the back; wavy, curly or parted coat; all bites other than scissors bite; monorchidism and cryptorchidism.

References for the Pomeranian Owner

General Source

> The American Kennel Club
> 51 Madison Avenue
> New York, New York 10010

Books

> General:
>> *The Complete Dog Book*—AKC
>> *International Encyclopedia of Dogs*—Dangerfield &
>> Howell
>> *Your Family Dog*—Riddle

> Breeding:
>> *How to Breed Dogs*—Whitney
>> *Inheritance of Coat Color in Dogs*—Little
>> *Joy of Breeding Your Own Show Dog*—Seranne
>> *Successful Dog Breeding*—Walkowicz & Wilcox

Obedience and Training:
Beyond Basic Dog Training—Bauman
Complete Book of Dog Obedience—Saunders
Dog Problems—Benjamin
Koehler Method of Dog Training—Koehler
Mother Knows Best: The Natural Way to Train Your Dog—Benjamin
New Knowledge of Dog Behavior—Pfaffenberger
Novice, Open and Utility Courses—Saunders
Successful Dog Training, Guide to—Pearsall

Structure and Movement:
Dog Anatomy, Illustrated—Way
Dogs in Action—Lyon
Dogsteps—Elliot

Dog Shows:
Dog Judges' Handbook—Tietjen
Successful Dog Showing, Guide to—Forsyth

Veterinary:
Complete Book of Dog Care—Whitney
Dog Owner's Encyclopedia of Veterinary Medicine—Hart
Dog Owner's Home Veterinary Handbook—Carlson & Griffin
Canine Clinic—Clarke

Out-of-Print Breed Books

Our Friend the Pomeranian—Johns
Show Pomeranians—Ives & Thomson
The Popular Pomeranian—Parker
Pet Pomeranian—Ricketts
This Is the Pomeranian—Spirer
The Complete Pomeranian—Denlinger
The New Complete Pomeranian—Ricketts